So You Want to Be The Master?

So You Want to Be The Master?

Maponga Joshua III "Vhudzijena"

iUniverse, Inc.
New York Lincoln Shanghai

So You Want to Be the Master?

iUniverse books may be ordered through booksellers or by contacting:

iUniverse
2021 Pine Lake Road, Suite 100
Lincoln, NE 68512
www.iuniverse.com
1-800-Authors (1-800-288-4677)

Because of the dynamic nature of the Internet, any Web addresses or links contained in this book may have changed since publication and may no longer be valid.

The views expressed in this work are solely those of the author and do not necessarily reflect the views of the publisher, and the publisher hereby disclaims any responsibility for them.

ISBN: 978-0-595-45567-6 (pbk)
ISBN: 978-0-595-69543-0 (cloth)
ISBN: 978-0-595-89870-1 (ebk)

Printed in the United States of America

CONTENTS

ACKNOWLEDGEMENTS

Almighty God: To the uncaused cause through whom we all have become, to Him who has no shadow and resides in wisdom the Maker of time, space and people, Yahweh, I thank you and I remain blessed.

Tribe: To the tribe of the Mapongas, vana Mukanya, Shoko, Hwiramiti, Mbereka, Dzinza rokwaNhokwara, vana vaMuchena zvizukurubvi zvaNyakunhuhwa, Shoko yeMbire to Joshua I Munyuki Maponga your wisdom, songs and teachings will live with me for a lifetime. Paul Fortune and the Fortune tribe, you gave me a shoulder to lean on during my ministry in Swaziland; Z and Myzoe Magagula, you were always there to help in times of need.

Family: Dad and Mum, Mr L and Mrs L Maponga, you never gave up on me and your prayers have kept me going. Patrick, my brother, you gave me hope when all was dark. This also extends to my sisters, Anna, Memory and Omega including Leo and Seth when all I needed was your prayers. Uncle Mike and Maiguru MaiDevi I thank you for shedding the gospel light and leading examples which I still sustain. To the rest of my uncles and aunts for the long nights spent at 144 Bikita early morning farm work, such survival skills are add on to my life. Lagoje; Thembekile, Shamiso and Tafara Maponga, out of our experience in the snows of London and the heat of Durban, what came out today is what you have contributed. From the time God sent you into my life I have never been the same again. The times we have spent as a family are priceless.

Teachers: Mr Mazambara my Primary School Headmaster, taking 'strong measures' and teaching to study until I sweat for blood, I remain thankful and this includes Pastor JM Nxumalo for the firm hand of discipline. Exclusively, Mrs Mlothwa and Mrs Siwardi for the morning devotions; Mr B Ncube, Ndaba Makhubalo for the strong scientific bias, I can still hear you reciting the Atomic charts; Mrs Dube, Mrs Ncube, Ms Becky Hawkinson, Ndimande, Ray Ngwenya, Ms Watson and Dr G. Basaninyenzi for the English classes and introduction into English and literature; Mrs Kengere for the geographic mind. Dr Z Ncube, Dr Obed Dube, Dr Z Mathema Dr Musvosvi, Dr H Mafu, Dr S Mfune, you were God send to minister to me in many ways. Mrs S Muze, the late, when I could not trust myself, you trusted God to shape me into what I am today.

Church: Kelvin Church, you make a wonderful congregation and the best memories of worship in Johannesburg are with you. Elder Mandla Msimang and Sipho Makhubela, you came handy to assist where possible.

Friends and Colleagues: To My friends and colleagues Gcina and Nhlapo; Ntombekhaya Fani Sarhili for the keen ear, timely advice, foresight into possibilities keep up the good work for I am sincerely thankful. Mthunzi 'Zazu'Mthimhkulu your continuous unwavering support over the years is noticed. Don Marandure your friendly honesty; Simbarashe Charumbira for the constant reminder that we stand on holy ground; Balindi Sanqele, Thuli I am blessed by your presence.

To this end, Prof. Modimowabarwa Hendrick Kanyane writing has not been difficult with you. As the Chief Editor of this book, you are continuously professing knowledge in the corridors of power. Under your watchful eye I will write again. You made difficult seems so simple and pleasurable. Thabo Moabi I owe allegiance for adding wings on this project and Charles Morrisson for his leap of faith on the same project. Katie Eagan our Publishing Services Associate for your prompt wise responses and the team @ iUniverse, Inc. you are the best. The list is endless, Bravo.

FOREWORD

This book is constructed of great thoughts profoundly put together to address the issues of life in the twenty-first century, whether they are socioeconomic, political, psychological, business-related, or spiritual. In this book, dynamic maxims drawn from theology, mathematics, business, jurisprudence, accounting, psychology, and the natural sciences are all pulled together to illustrate the theoretical and pragmatic bases of our lives. The two sciences, social and natural, will meet so that we may discover the master: an ideal cherished by all.

My responsibility during the write up of this manuscript was to validate facts and respond to queries posed by the publisher. This afforded me the opportunity to critically read this book. Guess what? My lifestyle has changed to that of the master—from ordinary to extraordinary—when dealing with current sophisticated issues of life. This has saved me from a lot of the blunders and mistakes of life I used to commit from time to time. If you don't believe me, I invite you to come and see who I am. If you are too far away to come and see me, I encourage you to begin to read all of the chapters contained in this book. The chapters are arranged systematically. You have to read them in the correct order, all the way to the end, to become a true master in your own right.

I have never seen a book on theology or business that addressed all of the important facets of life. These facets are: privacy, effort, development, action, selfishness, sympathy, philosophical fallacies, service, direction, and, most important, joy. This book addresses all one of them.

Chapter 10 of *Doctor Luke in the Holy Writ* sees the light of day in this book. When read in tandem with this book, it becomes crystal clear and meaningful, providing steps to recover, repackage, and sustain a broken soul during the current tough days of our lives. If you really want to be a master in your own right, try this book.

To God be the glory!
Kanyane MH, Professor of Public Administration
Editorial Desk

PREFACE

While reading many books that deal with management, I was strongly persuaded to write one myself. Many writers seem to be scared to address the spirituality of a businessperson as a source of moral ethics. Too much emphasis is placed on techniques to get ahead of your competitors, and too little on how to develop lasting relationships with your clients and colleagues. Your religion and faith has a direct impact on your moral ethics. What we see in the boardroom is but a reflection of the deity in the closet.

As you believe, so you behave. This is the most important tool in building and maintaining your business integrity. Issues of faith can't be downplayed by formulas and research strategies. Let every professional take a minute to think: What picture do I paint in the minds of my employees, customers, and competitors? At the thought of you, let them have a picture of a truthful and fair man.

You need to constantly confront your demons of materialism, greed, and apathy. Love people, and view them as your greatest assets. To master the human psyche and harness these wild horses is a skill every professional should strive to attain. This skill was not part of your school curriculum, because your teachers presumed that your mother and father had taught you at home. Some of these traits are so simple yet so critical that it becomes a risk to establish relationships without clear knowledge of them.

Have you ever wondered why some people think that you are offensive, coarse, or unlikable? Does it bother you that your first impression doesn't strike the right chord in the hearts of your prospects? This is interior design, bringing the inside outside. The arrangements of the furniture of your heart and the cutlery of your brain will show in your outward dealing.

Holding a degree in philosophy topped up with CET (Construction Entrepreneurial Training) and ILO (International Labour Organisation) initiative to develop local consultants and support for emerging contractors and manufacturers, I am qualified social entrepreneur having abilities which range from creative intellectual power to pragmatic innovative thinking. Hence I have a keen interest in in-depth thinking, behavioural patterns, and paradigmatic shifts in mindsets. Given this background, I have successfully managed major brands in South Africa and have earned a reputation, both locally and internationally, due to excellent spirited and entrepreneurial presentations. I believe in ethical virtue which must be the moral foundation across the cultural fields. If the global village is to materialize, then let 'ubuntu' (the preservation of the human spirit) be the moral law that will gorven its citizens, hence this book.

With these experiences that I have gone through, my intention is to share with the professional some fundamental truths and values that have been tested by time and are practical across religious lines. It doesn't matter what religion you follow—learning is linear. This is an alternative look at biblical principles that can be applied to life and social relationships.

In your desire to go out and tame the world start off by taming your inner self. Like an experienced ox on the plough, you will walk on the right and tame the young, energetic one on the left. Together, you will become productive and disciplined, like team players on the playing field.

Be a good winner and a good loser. Sincerely rejoice in the successes of your counterparts. Learn how to climb the ladder of success, and learn how to fall. Master the art of getting up and doing again. That resilience will eternally mark the difference between masters and servants.

Moses and the Burning Bush

Being a master is an act in the presence of God; it is an act of faith done under divine supervision. It is using ordinary tools with God. Success in privacy (like that of Moses) will show itself as grand success, as of the leader of a nation in dry lands with harsh conditions. Mastery is a secret of success that puts your life a cut above the rest. In the wilderness of life, people are looking for extraordinary people. God has to call for your attention, request that you take off your shoes, remind of you the ground on which you stand, give you instructions, change your paradigm, and finally give you a mission in life.

With a dead stick in his hand, Moses made a lifeless thing come to life. Why live life in a lifeless environment and blame yourself when surrounded by death? You should be the master, in partnership with God, and make the lifeless sticks come alive. Cast them on the ground, and see what potential is inside of ordinary tools. While standing on holy ground, you can cooperate with God to transform things, people, and the environment.

The snake, writhing on the desert sand, needs you to hold it by the tail. There is a need for a master who can tame these volatile desert serpents, changing them to harmless yet useful sticks. You want to be that master.

I wrote this book for myself. I want to be remembered for having lived a better life and having made this world a better place.

INTRODUCTION

The title "master" belongs to those who have mastered disciplines, those who can control difficult situations at ease with skill and self-discipline, and those who possess power that is built on knowledge and experience. It belongs to those who act on the basis of information and to those whose attitudes are founded on confidence. Masters of life experience living a moment before it becomes reality and are attracted to the deeper issues of life. Being a master is a journey into control and power; it is a discipline that sacrifices temporary pleasure for long-term goals.

Being a master should not be an ideal to long for, but a lifestyle to emulate and live. You will rub shoulders with those who are surviving, but you, the master, must *live*. I challenge you to laugh until your ribs hurt, to cry until you feel your tear glands are empty, and to love until there is nothing left to give. A master must respond to the call of making the best of every instant, building the best of the minute at hand.

If this is your desire and you find yourself in a battle of the mind, struggling with core issues of ethics and control, you were my motivation for the penning of this work. The reader will be exposed to the ultimate and be challenged to visualize and accept this as an achievable reality.

The small acts of sensitivity springing from an ethical heart make the world a better place. While multitudes wait for awe-inspiring events in their lives, this work encourages you to perform small miracles in your immediate environment.

Feeling lost and looking for something to read to fill my need for control during a dark point of my life, I went to the book shop, and I found these books that address issues that are burning in the conscience of our society:

- *Dianetics:* helping people to define goals and have enthusiasm
- *Yoga:* exercises that help people to be in touch with the energies around them, mental power over matter, an appeal that the mind can conquer anything (though it still leaves lots of questions about death), spiritual journeys in search of one's soul, divides human life into a jungle that must be explored and instigates a search for the lost self
- *The Secrets of Ancient Wisdom:* visiting the past, looking for answers to the present, investigating lifestyles and seeking solutions from past habits and practices
- *Magic Thinking:* performing outward magic with a spark within your mind
- *You Think, So You Are:* the power of thought over behavior
- *Start Now:* time management strategies
- *How to Get from Where You Are to Where You Want to Be:* avenues and direction of investment of effort and resources (Jack Canfield)
- *How to Get Rich:* making the effort to make money, the capitalistic appeal on how to get to the top
- *Where Have Leaders Gone?:* in search for the true meaning of leadership
- *Think Like a Billionaire:* liberating thoughts into an attitude of change and wealth creation
- *The Money Goddess:* investment strategies for women, encouragement for women to achieve financial clout
- *Habits of Highly Effective People:* a classic by Stephen R. Covey on being effective in a corporate setting by being at peace with oneself
- *Emotional Intelligence:* positive thinking tips from Goleman and TV show guru Dr. Phil McGraw
- *Leading from the Front:* visible leadership skills

- *Hands-off Manager*
- *The Origin of Wealth:* starting at the beginning and finding the true source of wealth
- *Turning Silver to Gold:* activities that seem inconsequential but could work to help individuals attain results
- *Investment Strategies:* how to play the money game
- *Building Brands:* growing products and services to make a lasting impression on your clients
- *Change Management*
- *Who Moved My Cheese?*
- *Putting Your Strength to Work:* marketing techniques or business planning tools
- Biographies of economic giants: Branson, Trump, Bill Gates
- Project management kits, "Dummies" grammar tools, small packs of wisdom

So You Want to Be the Master is an offering to the soul. Stop theorizing about life, get your hands into the mud, and *do*. This book is a practical guide, made easy by a parallel story to help readers see where they are and anticipate their journeys, helping them know what to do when confronted with a multifaceted maze of relationships.

Some stalwarts have failed, leaving bad examples and discouraging many from walking this "road less traveled." In this book, you will be the example. You will master the art of leaving your footprint, registering your existence, and leaving a trace of influence and impact.

Chapter One

Master of Privacy

There are times when academic preparation is not sufficient. Your teachers and parents never told you some of these things.

And behold, a certain lawyer stood up and tempted Him.
(Luke 10:25)

A teacher of the law came to question the master teacher. He had been through the curriculum of legal preparation, and he had not seen the word "neighbor." In all his reading, he failed to see the verbs, or "doing words." Life is not about nouns; it is about action. The man found comfort in the dark. He did not want to be seen or recognized, and in the midst of all these uncertainty, he knew who had answers to his questions.

"Behold!" announces a grand, visible presence. All of this is outer strength hiding a subterranean huddle of internal deficits. All of us conceal our ugly intentions behind expensive cars, suits, sunglasses, facial creams, and perfumes.

The reek is still there. Like Naaman of old, go to the river and wash. Other moments will find us hiding behind others, camouflaging our lack of knowledge with others' excellence; monotonous and tired brains will surround their dullness with deep thinkers; complex books and gadgets will obscure shallowness. Stand alone, and you can stand with others. Persuade yourself, and you can convince others.

There is a time in life when you must not be seen by anybody or be identified for what you have achieved. Life is never masked by proliferation. Books and accolades are not vaccines for tears and trouble. There are times when darkness is comfort, like when you are in a mess, after a mistake, on the verge of embarrassing yourself, and you are sure that your preparation is not sufficient for the task at hand.

Some expectations will exhaust your intelligence, expose you as deficient, and render you incompetent. What do you do when the challenge was not part of your assignment, or the decision was not part of your job? What do you do when the decision can't be taken home for consultation? Truth needs to be integrated into life so that decisions become instinctive and spontaneous. Your inner self needs to be familiar with decisions, rendering you ready at all times to make the right choice. The law of cause and effect is important here.

In this life full of diaries, connecting flights, laptops, and endless chains of meetings for corporate professionals, be sure that you don't bury yourself in business and disregard yourself. Step out of the crust of preoccupation and unearth a place of your own privacy. These are moments of no television, newspapers, cell phones, or iPods. It is a time for reflection and introspection.

Rearranging the furniture of your inner life and dusting the cobwebs from outstanding assignments is a paramount virtue. Ask yourself questions and interrogate your motives, analyze your behavior and revisit your tangential relationships, marital or extramarital, and inspect your mannerisms in the theater of life.

Our learned friend the lawyer stood up to tempt and interrogate Jesus. Why would he find it easier to cross-examine Jesus instead of cross examining himself? External veneers always seem easy; it is easier to remove a splinter in someone else's eye than to remove a log in your own eye. Isn't it better to do an operation on myself first before performing a gruesome operation of destruction while obstructed by my own weaknesses? The presence of the log is humor; how did you even see it?

Behind the big log, the worst failure in life is the internal being. When we have given up within, there is little that can be done outside. The opposite is equally rewarding. When you have overcome your demons within and the trumpet of success echoes inside you, nothing can put you down.

The lawyer should have stood with himself shoulder to shoulder, faced his demons, and argued his strength before arm wrestling with the supernatural. Lawyers build bad habits of always winning arguments. Often they seem to have won the case and lost the truth. So it is in life when you crush someone and you win the discussion but lose a friend. Life is not about winning and losing. Win some, lose some. Fight some, and let others go. Select your battles and opponents carefully. If it is in business, take risks, but calculate and manage your risks. Don't overexpose yourself. Success can be measured when an investor asks questions and find solutions to challenging problems ahead of time. To be surprised and claim ignorance over unforeseen circumstances is a recipe for bankruptcy.

In public speaking, as in marriage, not all you say is important. You can't turn your home into a police station or a courtroom. Children can't be disciplined for everything that is wrong. Timing is everything.

There are times when the sleeping dogs must be left to lie. Let the birds fly over your head at will, but not too often, lest they make their nests in the chambers of your thoughts. Like an eagle, high in the spacious skies, use your sight to identify prey.

Look critically at the profession you are in, and beware that your strength could be your weakness. Move gracefully from wearing one hat to another. A mother can be a wife, a boss at work, a team member at the local club, and a deaconess at church. Wisdom is the ability to adapt for relevance.

A nurse will look at everybody as a patient, and a manager will think all are employees; a millionaire will presume that all are beggars in search of his money. You might end up running away from the people hoping to save your life when there is no one chasing you.

Don't become a robot exhibiting antisocial behavior. It is humiliating to be told your armpits smell, your breath could fumigate for tropical mosquitoes, or your socks could infect your neighbors with flu virus, and you can't tell. Before they vote to put you in quarantine and spray air freshener upon your departure, save yourself the humiliation by being critical of yourself. Be frank, and spare no details. Repair or demolition is your choice. You are building internal resilience.

When entering a new state of affairs, don't rush for the microphone and the oratory desk. There is no supermarket that manufactures and sells marriage. The vows are taken while people are standing. The good counsel is that one should sit down to learn. Even in business, the first-time education, whether formal or informal, is the mill that produces active participants that foster change and development.

The world is not looking for population or numbers but agents of change. In brief, they are looking for you, the master, to foster change and development. The greater part of the population causes problems. You need to decide to be the solution bearer and not the trouble maker—to be a blessing with your presence. If you are not part of the solution, you are surely the cause (or part) of the problem.

Why would you do something and leave no mark? In every occupation, let your hands show excellence, seal your presence. Let your scrutinizing eyes expose every detail. In your hand, let there be no negligence; let your implementation be complete without need of supervision.

The reality of life is that some things are never "by the book" but they need skills to handle. You are on the battlefield, armed or civilian. Challenges never respect personalities. The rich and poor die, the educated and simple both get sick, children get pregnant, and houses are repossessed by commercial banks. Accidents happen, and life is constantly at risk; you had better be on guard. Like the soldier in Ephesians 6, beware of your naked sports. An armor not fully utilized exposes the weak areas, and a wall that is not joined together makes a door. "Put on the whole armor" (Ephesians 6:10–20).

After you have been with yourself, you must find the voice within that you can talk to. I am a Christian, so I talk to the Holy Spirit to align my concerns, and I have internalized the scriptures so that I may use them to formulate opinions, meeting my problems head-on. Divine things need divine insights and apparatus. Tools are everything they will enhance your task, make you professional, protect you from injuries, and save your time. Apply the right attitude to a situation, and your altitude will surely change.

Some places need you to be a disciple rather than a lawyer. Admit that you don't know everything in life. Some of us married Mrs. Right or Mr. Right; the danger, though, is that they are right all the time. Like Moses of old, there are times when we need to take off our shoes, for the ground on which we stand is holy (Exodus 3:1–6).

Not everything is common in life. There are places, people, and situations that demand your spiritual attitude. Some might demand your knees, or your hands, or your head. It is crucial to understand that you need to take off your shoes at times, as you walk on holy ground, which is unfamiliar turf.

Opportunities and blessings are forfeited when you are too casual and you underestimate the value of the moment. There are times when you are there, right there. If you said the right thing, it could change your life forever. It is that moment when you can almost hear Jesus praying in the garden, but then you fall asleep.

Masters need to harness the moment; one wrong action, word, or comment could jeopardize and compromise a deal. A silly slip of the tongue could swing a case and implicate the innocent. Be a master, and take nothing for granted. Every action must maximize your impact.

Yes, we could have been here a hundred times, but today is out of the ordinary. Regular places are visited by the supernatural in theophanic encounters. Even if the divine hand is invisible, the impact will remain, and the benefit is in the long run. At times, even your children will reap the fruits of your actions. Our previous understanding and persuasion must be circumscribed by the ritual of learning. I come here to learn and not to prove, to sit and not to stand. You could have stood in court many times, but when you get to Jesus, sir, sit down.

Find your place in the classroom of learning. Whatever the challenges of life are, if you can't adapt, you die. Every organization that is doing business has to Plan, Do, and Adjust (PDA). If you have not changed your way of doing things in the last fifty years, you are slowly dying. People should not pride themselves for being unteachable, their stern stances unmoved by facts. You hear them say, "No one will convince me, no matter what you do or say," but an objective outlook will always be fresh in the reality of the present.

Brands have to evolve, or they fossilize. Those who stand too often and don't take time to sit down will soon learn that they stand for nothing, and mortification will show them the chair by force. Here's some good advice: stand next to your chair.

There is a time for everything under the sun, the wise man advises. There is a time to sit down, a time to stand, a time to learn, and a time to challenge the status quo.While it might seem that our time is taken up with motivation courses, feel-good workshops, and pain-killer religions, you must understand the correct foundation of drive in life. It's the walking of hot coals or unleashing of brain power in the emptiness of kinetics and calisthenics. They who have learned to sit down and learn will stand to be counted. The foundation is knowledge, experience, and humility. To everyone who has sat down: yes, you will stand. Prudence will not allow temporary solutions to permanent problems. The ultimate posture ("Behold! I stand!") should clear all doubt, fear, and uncertainty, validating your time to speak and be seen. When you stand, stand; and when you sit, sit. Emotionalism and the misguided expression of assertiveness are the playing fields of inadequate idiots.

There are chairs that prepare people for podiums. Never ridicule a man or a woman who is sitting down; they are at the feet of the skilled, and they are being educated. A farmer sharpening his axe has learned the twinge of working with a blunt axe. The result is blisters, broken skin, and wasted strength. Sit down and sharpen your axe, and you will hack down a good number of trees with less strength. It saves you time.

You are wise if you inspect your tools. Be content if you sit to sharpen your tool. A sharp tool in the hand of God can achieve much more in less time. There is no need to torture people with a bucket of words, trying to express a teaspoonful of sense or fulfill the English proverb that says "Empty buckets make the most noise." The idea of "sitting down" is a positive attitude toward learning.

True strength is that which is within. When you know who you are, what you made of, and where you are going, it is the firm pillar of steel that anchors your soul. When these steel structures stand, we all can behold the results in people like Martin Luther King (Martin Luther King was a German monk and Protestant reformer who lived from 1483 to 1546. Martin Luther King Jr. was an African American famous for peaceful demonstrations during the U.S. civil rights movement in the mid-1900s), Nelson Mandela, and Mahatma Gandhi. As I speak, I know; and as I know, I live. That which stands inside must be taller than you. So firm must be your posture that even when you are sitting, they will think you are standing.

To oppose me is a war on your scruples, to stand with me is to become a comrade in arms. When masters like Gandhi, Luther King, and Mandela stand, we sit down … but note that they had to sit in order to stand. Standing, therefore, is a summary of your sitting experience. Good speakers are good listeners. When you sit at the feet of Jesus, you will stand before the kings and rulers.

Reflections

- As a couple, devise methods of self-critique.
- Let every family "visit the dissecting table and remove the tumors."
- Society and your community need to hear your song.
- Always think globally and act locally.
- List your role models.
- What drives your winning or fear of losing?
- How do you manage risk?
- What is the most important investment in your business?
- How often do you talk to yourself?
- Note your "naked sports."
- How do you approach new areas and experiences?

- How open are you to change?
- Why do women give birth—for pleasure or for survival?
- What do you think about human dynamics?
- Check your tools (education, emotions, etc.). How sharp are these tools?

Applications

- Find time for private reflection.
- Identify your weaknesses.
- Openly criticize yourself.
- Never pretend to know; gear up to learn.
- Win from within, then fight from without.
- Stand with yourself.
- It is okay to lose at times.
- Take calculated risks.
- Save your strength for bigger battles.
- People are more important than all machines and money.
- Align your inner voice with solid principles.
- Be ready to fight; you are at war.
- Utilize all of your ammunition: mental, physical, social, and spiritual. Protect every part of your body. Spiritual things are spiritually discerned.
- Prepare a career advancement program.
- Deliberately let other opportunities go while you sharpen yourself.
- When you are sure of your ground, stand with confidence. Find those areas where you are currently strong, and grow the turf to other water-clogged areas.
- Claim the soggy lands, nurture your chances, and master your weaknesses.

And behold, a certain lawyer stood up and tempted him.
(Luke 10:25)

This world is waiting to see you standing on your feet to challenge way things are. Don't settle for trivia and be comforted by past triumphs. Refrain from sitting at the feet of shallow wells, like Nicodemus. Before you sink into tedium, sit down, sharpen your ears, and invigorate your mind. This is the first step to rising from indistinctness into a profile of success. Sit down. We will wait until you are ready to stand.

CHAPTER TWO

MASTER OF EFFORT

Master, what shall I do to inherit the kingdom of heaven?
(Luke 10:25)

These are the sayings of people who have given up:

- I have had enough of him or her.
- I can't take it anymore.
- This has gone too far.
- This is way out of line.
- I am being taken for granted.
- I need to teach someone a lesson.
- I am running out of patience.
- I am sick and tired of the dirty tricks.
- We need to do something.
- This is now subject to discipline.
- The message is falling on deaf ears.
- That is a sheer waste of time.
- That is a hopeless case.
- That's it. I said that's it.
- Get off my case. Get a life.

- Leave me alone. You don't understand.
- We are not on the same page.
- I am now officially off your case.
- You give over to the dogs.
- Is there anything more?
- I thought I had done it all.
- Beyond this, I can't help.
- This doesn't make sense at all.
- It seems too simple. There must be a catch.
- I have done all I can. What more can I do?
- Someone explain. Is there something I skipped?

The word "saying" indicates continuity and nonstop speech. Have you ever been in a place where you wished people would just shut up? I hope they did not feel the same way about you. We need to know how to punctuate our speech and use the grammatical elements correctly.

? question mark

! exclamation mark

, comma

" quotation mark

. full stop

In your quest to establish yourself, value knowledge above recognition. Question misinformation; beware of conversations crammed with hot air. Some minds can only hear their own voices; they are self-opinionated and crowded with caustic *self*, empty craniums filled with unawareness. Ask when you don't know, and pause when someone has something to say. Give credit when using other people's quotes, and after you have said what you want to say, be quiet. Start slowly, start at the beginning, speak, and when you reach the end, stop.

Some speeches are like airplanes that loiter in the skies and never land when the runway is clear; when you thought they were finished, they initiate another takeoff. It's not in the volume of words that we measure the impact of a speech; we don't glory in the sanctity of perspiration. Speech is a powerful tool. In the hand of a master, it has eternal impact. Through the tongue, lives are changed, decisions are altered, and behavior is corrected. Every master needs to master the power of words and build the broken walls of society with words, creating an environment where relationships can flourish.

Relationships are not disposable diapers; they are more like cotton diapers that need to be washed and then reused. Don't throw out the baby with the bathwater; redeem the esteemed and discard the ineffectual. Content and context must preside over mere talk.

There are masters in most fields of life. Those who nurture their individuality and fitness of mind become reputable in their fields. It is by these masters that we are challenged to enhance ourselves and aspire to move above mediocrity.

A good master is priceless, whether he or she is a maharishi, mentor, counselor, tutor, guru, coach, or adviser. In life, you need a reliable sounding board where you can express your uncertainty and use the master's experience to evade common blunders.

When standing side by side with a master, you are at the border of your merit. The desire is to immigrate to the land of your master. Having come this far, it is sad if you turn back. A man was promised riches if he could swim three kilometers; he swam one and a half kilometers, got tired, and swam back. It takes the same amount of energy to retreat, so invest it in completion. Learn from the traditional Zulu proverb, "A wise bird makes its nest with other birds' feathers." Learn from the experience of others.

Here is a man who wants to do something, but what should he do? Identify a task for him to execute, and he promptly changes from speech to activity. He wants to do. He is a man of action.

There are times when doing is more helpful than talking: activities of growth, activities of love, activities of discipline, mercy, forgiveness, focus, patience, success, and humility. The list goes on. Find these activities, and indulge your spirit in turning weaknesses into strongholds of power. Never should you pride yourself on an ailment as if it is ecstasy. Weeds in your garden must be uprooted, and only superior crops should grow. Make space by eradicating wastes of energy. Energy wasted on nothing is regrettable, and the moments frivolously blown away by purposelessness are gone forever.

Find time to the core business. If you are in a relationship, talking is not as important as doing. Pay your dues, and fulfill your obligations. Optional proclivity can never share a seat with compulsory contractual obligation. It's amazing that people make so much money and will not hesitate to spend exorbitant sums on things other than the core relationship. I have seen people divorce with millions in their accounts. Just get down to *doing*. Go on vacation. Look after each other. Use the money to make the relationship work. Let wealth labor for you, instead of you working for it. What does it profit a man if he gains the entire world and loses his own soul?

Good strategies will die on the table unless they are converted into actions. Pillows are fat with dreams that never saw the dawn of day. "I wish" is a raw prayer of delusion. The difference between success and failure is action. Act upon the activities of development.

Keep focused on positive activities; there is a grand reward. To inherit a kingdom is much more than toil and profit. This can't be achievement or luck; this is providence. This attainment surely supersedes all personal sacrifices and seeming loss. When you stand at this acme, you think of all but loss. Those who do have inherited empires and kingdoms.

How do you establish your empire? Look at your home, your relationship, your job, and your business; these are areas you need to not only influence but also command. Victory in these seemingly negligible areas will vitalize your winning instincts, leading to new ventures.

Shakespeare wrote, "Some are born great, some achieve greatness and some have greatness thrust upon them." Three groups are found here.

Those that inherit, those that work hard to achieve, and yet others who just happen to be at the right place at the right time. No matter what the method, greatness is the ultimate consequence for all three. All of us can be great. Shakespeare advocates inclination by blood. Harvest greatness from the sweat of your brow, your network, and your lucrative close associations.

Kings and masters don't ask for respect; neither should they demand respect from subordinates. They earn respect by their behavior. Let your conduct signal authority and arouse respect. Those who run empires can't meet their expenses without having good reputations. You must protect your reputation at all costs; so important is your repute that you can withdraw credit from it. A master's word is like a dog on a leash. The wise man Solomon adds "it is the glory of God to conceal a thing: but the honour of kings is to search out a matter. As the heavens are high and the earth is deep so the hearts of the kings are unsearchable" (Proverbs 25:2-3).

It's not easy turning a commoner into a prince or princess. When beggars become rulers, learning is critical, so that they do not go back to where they began. The progress from a student to a master is a trying one filled with observation and emulation. A student needs to live with gurus and be a co-owner together with a master in the empire of facts.

Romans 8:15–17 has this to say:

> *For ye have not received the spirit of bondage again to fear; but ye have received the Spirit of adoption, whereby we cry, Abba, Father.*
>
> *The Spirit itself beareth witness with our spirit, that we are the children of God:*
>
> *And if children, then heirs; heirs of God, and joint-heirs with Christ; if so be that we suffer with [him], that we may be also glorified together.*

If you are willing to walk where the masters have walked, you'll have the blessing of being under experienced instruction. Crosses give birth to crowns.

It's not always up to you to accomplish success; at other times, it's what others do for you. Instead of asking, "What can I do?" you can also ask, "What can you do for me?" or "What have you done for me?" In theology classes, we teach salvation by faith, not works. We are not saved by what we do; we are saved by what Jesus has done for us. By the time we *do*, it is him working in us.

We do good things not to be saved, but because we are saved. External actions are exhibits of the heart and its conversion. For this reason, good people will be in hell. The motivation for action is self-indulgence and clearing of conscience. Actions that don't have a sense of a higher moral obligation can fulfill but a minimal space.

A young man had some fish and bread, but in the hands of Jesus, it fed many; a little can do much when placed in supernatural hands. This is the student and the master at the service of mankind. Transferring all he had into the creative hands of Jesus, he ended up with the question, "How many baskets of leftovers do we have after five thousand people have eaten?"

The people in a relationship must meet in the middle and contribute by acting. Each party needs to empty itself and be submissive in order to learn. Backgrounds and previous lives are skeletons in closets that only masters who are equipped to solve difficult problems can handle. You are going to be that master. Look at the quadratic equation:

If $a + b = c + d$
If $a = 3$ and $b = 4$ $c = 5$ $d = 2$
Then $a + b = c + d$ which is a (3) + b (4) = c (5) + d (2)
Therefore $a + b = 7 = c + d = 7$

If you can solve such a complex equation, why not take this principle into crisis management and learn to look at both sides of the same coin? When arguments start, let the masters calculate and balance the equation. Husband and wives, bosses and employees—it doesn't matter which position you are in. You are the master.

Masters always strive for cloud nine, which is Jerusalem. The story of the Samaritan starts off in Jerusalem, a city of Salem referred to as a city of peace. Hence masters should start their arguments from this peaceful threshold. This must moderate all dialogue in your empire, let alone heaven. "Heaven" here could mean a place where all is well: no pain, no war, no disease, no funerals. Masters need to share, act, and make an impact—not with violence, but from a premise of peace.

It would be astounding to see tigers play with goats, lions share pastures with sheep, children putting their hands in a cobra's nest, and bears and kids sleeping together. Look around: there must be a master nearby who can tame the wildest and create an environment where the weak and strong are together in peace. If you should become the leader of a large team, master the trick.

As a master, you can walk on fire, and it will not hurt you; you can drink poison, and it will not harm you; spend a night with lions, and they will become vegetarians. If that becomes possible, then you have become a master. Develop a strong sense of ecological intelligence. Find the common denominator, and strike a balance at all times. Being robust and arrogant and pushing people with power doesn't build you; rather, it destroys you. Be a master; be part of the great ecosystem. Increase functionality and profitability.

Be full of possibilities. Teach and tame bears so they will gobble grass; make tigers into eaters of fruit. Managing people is a dynamic skill that you need to master, until the most hostile of people become like tame oxen in your hands. This skill will render you powerful, and wisdom will protect you. Be part of the solution instead of being part of the problem.

Masters make things work. Marriages, homes, and jobs can be made into heavens. Masters create places where kings and queens stay. A foreman will never be promoted until he has trained someone to assume his job; maybe that is the reason you are still in the same position. Be the master. Multiply yourself. Plant your vision and goals in the heads of those who work with you. Be the master of the things that God has allowed to be under your auspices, for as you are held responsible, you will give account.

I have seen marriages, jobs, and companies that have been turned into prisons and little hells: full of restriction, sentences, court appeals, penalties, judgments, and a lot of heat that burns the occupants. I also have seen husbands and wives who no longer kiss but instead shake hands, people who are in their homes for their children, and those who work because they need the money. As a master, when your empire involves people at this level, be warned that you are at nominal strength and will not be able to achieve results equal to your capacity.

A master will turn chaos into a cosmos, formlessness into form and order. A master will shout light into darkness, hangs stars in the skies, separates waters, causes plants to come out of speech, and allow for variety. A master will also call light day and darkness, night. Masters will balance the atmospheric pressure, regulate the seasons, and speak, transforming nothing into something. Faith is a must for masters.

Believing in your choices, believe in your employees, and believe in people; believe in your spouse and in the partner at your office. Speak, and it will become real. Believe in them, and they will perform. The best inventors and stalwarts were rejects in the hands of idle tutors. The same brains, in the hands of masters, become unsung heroes and heroines; mothers and grandmothers dare to say, "My son or my daughter is not worthless." A master's word of encouragement becomes fuel for inventions. Steam engines, fluorescent lights, IT gadgets, Windows programs, aerodynamics, hydraulics, floatation, calibrations, synthetics, and philosophy—all are at the hands of masters.

All things are connected to business. Society and family are deliberately positioned, seemingly at odds with one another, but in essence, integral. Look carefully, and draw associations between aspects of your life. It will be a joy to place each item into perspective, to see the relationship between cause and effect.

Be able to change situations instead of being changed by them. Stand on the deck amidst the boisterous sea, and shout, "Peace! Be still!" Find lonely women at the well, and leave them managing a church. Find dead companies, three days rotting, and roll away the stones, and shout, "Life!" Those possessed will be restored. Funeral processions and business liquidations will be turned into hymns of praise.

The paralyzed and infirm who have lain ill for thirty-eight years will be able to rise, pick up their mats, and walk. Masters teach, masters heal, masters minister, masters rebuke, masters clean up, and masters sacrifice. Masters have upper rooms of revelation and valleys of prayer; they also have crosses to carry and death to face, but true masters never die. They will rise again from their graves.

Sunday is on the way. Jesus died on Friday, and the arrival of Sunday is the arrival of good news of victory. In the midst of adversity, a master should have hope that there will be a brighter day when what are called myths will be accepted as facts. The fact that the masters see it doesn't mean that other people will see it in the same way too. But let the master have faith that Sunday, the day of the resurrection of truth, is on the way. Sacrifice might seem fruitless at the time of pain, but a seed well planted will not die. Masters have to struggle to make the community see what they see. It might take centuries for a type of ignorance to be cured, but that delay doesn't nullify projection and prophetic sight. Galileo is dead, and the world has officially been declared round. Jesus is dead, and the world is full of Christians. A true vision can never be destroyed.

When you, as a master, feel that you have done all you could, ask yourself, "What more can I do?" In times of crisis—divorce, unemployment, arrest, deportation, etc.—it is vital to combine your efforts with divine aid. When these moments arrive, you are becoming a master. Your decision will separate the wheat from the chaff. These moments demand extraordinary vigor, valor, and vim ("the three Vs"). They make you or break you. This is the river that common people can't cross, for masters are not ordinary, but they do ordinary things with a strange touch of wit.

At these moments, masters are aware that they are surrounded by a cloud of witnesses. They move from the sphere of people to the empire of angels. Masters operate on a higher level. If you argue with a master, you are wrong. They increase their altitude, beginning the bizarre, loving the unlovable, giving hope to the hopeless, talking to the dead, turning the other cheek, and going the extra mile. They know that it is a test of their power, tenacity, and endurance. The danger is in using physical power to solve physical problems. This only results in wars and sanctions.

It is true that we fight not against flesh and blood but against principalities and forces in high places. In the realm of the unseen, there is a war that has a direct link to the troubles and challenges you face in the visible world. There are things you have to do in the physical world that prepare and arm you for warfare in the invisible realm. The weaponry of this war is not carnal but spiritual. It is not a religious cliché but a reality you must face. The greatest of all wars ever fought is between your two ears. Forces of good and evil are hanging over your soul. You need to empower one of them, and your vote decides the outcome of the battle.

Masters use supernatural principles to solve physical problems, as in the great revolutions of our century: apartheid in South Africa championed by Nelson Mandela, passive resistance, the Indian nonviolent revolution and victory over the British empire, and the civil right movement in the United States of America. There is power in this principle. No guns and power can overcome a spirit that has touched the supernatural. The implements are timeless. Human hands can't control it; it is in the domain of angels.

Reflections

- How well do you rate yourself in the use of common sense?

- What message are you sending? What are you saying?

- How passionate are you about fixing the areas of your life that are falling apart? How passionate are you about personal change?

- Do you love yourself enough to implement changes that will give you a happier life?

- How are your relationships? What causes disputes in your relationships?
- What is the one thing that you desire to happen in your life?
- What myths do you have about your success?

Applications

- Identify possible mentors, and allocate time for growth.
- Learn to learn. Have the right attitude toward learning.
- Make the decision to listen while other talk.
- Evaluate your endurance and resilience.
- Learn from the experience of others. Observe and apply.
- Take your obligations seriously.
- Plan your action, and carry it out.
- Clarify your thoughts; it's essential if you want to convey them to others.
- Be credible at all times. Protect your reputation.
- Claim success in your life.

Master, what shall I do to inherit the kingdom of heaven?
(Luke 10:25)

Rise above the situations that press you down. Seek to view the unseen, hear the unheard, touch the untouchable. Here is an offer of inheritance: reach out beyond the common and strive to become a master. Turn all into heaven, and live there.

CHAPTER THREE

MASTER OF DEVELOPMENT

He said unto him, what is written in the law and how readest thou?
(Luke 10:26)

He said unto him—*spoken*
What is written?—*preserved*
What is written in the law?—*moral record*
How readest thou?—*interpretation*

For those who do public speaking, marketing, and presentations, here is another way of presenting things. First and foremost, look into what others have to say on the subject you're presenting. Establish the background from which you will derive your analysis. You are probably not the first person to discuss your given subject. Read widely, and then write down your thoughts. Internalize your thoughts and pinpoint the moral undertones in your message. It's only after going through this process that you can speak with conviction.

Everyone has a story to write and tell. A black race which studied Bantu education in Africa has not fully embraced reading and writing as tools for advancement. Many people last read books at college and will sail through jobs without ever reading to increase their understanding. The phrase, "If you want to hide it from the black man, write it down," offensive as it might seem, has some truth in it. It implies that we are not keen on fine details. Our comfort is in the superficial waters and bold letters on contracts.

In this day and age, when information has increased greatly, there is a written page at every turn. It is amazing how you still find people basking in the shadows of hearsay. It's all within reach, yet some will depend on others to read and then tell them. This circus is best seen at church, where people will convert their bibles into music instruments and never bother to read. The poor bishop, with little or archaic academic preparation, must struggle to be relevant to a generation that is plugged into technology.

One member of a church was asked, "What do you believe?"

He answered, "I believe what my church believes."

"And what does your church believe?"

He answered, "It believes what the pastor believes."

"And what does your pastor and the church believe?"

He answered, "They believe the same thing."

Don't just be a follower who will not question issues of life. Even worship must be done out of understanding.

You need to build a relationship with your books. In whatever field you are in, learn to always read and write. Contribute articles to journals and professional magazines. Write your findings, and bridge the gap of local content. Most of our history needs to be rewritten; it presents blacks as inferior and paints whites as saints who died for the right cause, and this is wrong.

Women are reduced to bearing children, working in the kitchens while their own children roam the streets like headless chickens, being hunted and gunned down like foxes in their own land. What sort of faith will keep us, as a people, together? Someone will say this is political, when it is actually a reality of life. How do you read? If people are fed the wrong information, they will never know and fully understand the gist of the matter. They might even make wrong choices and idolize the wrong gods.

I will not sit here and listen to bigots speak of a white Jesus and a black devil. Instead, we might need to start talking about a black Jesus and a white devil. Historical apartheid and racism toward black people might end up showing a different scenario, one of a black savior and white devils. Humans must not be classified by their skins, but by the fabric of their souls, regardless of creed or genealogy.

Looking at our history legacy, it must be written so that our people could locate their God. This would be the god who took them out of slavery and bondage. God led us through the wilderness and warmed us in the cold winter nights while we were on the trains to the gold mines. God fed us when we worked in the mines, when our land was snatched from our hands and our women were raped. There is a God the world doesn't know, but we know him.

"What is written?" Those who can write should write these monologues of the heart. Someone should write about broad-based black economic empowerment, contextualization, enculturation, indignity, social politics, the collapse of traditional houses, third-world economics, how investments are the false reality of banking, African politics, and power in the African psyche. Write about African inventions, parallels between culture and religion, medical survival of the African people, engineering, witchcraft, and magic. Lot of things happens at funerals; behaviors, mannerisms, rituals, and traditions (which way does the head of the dead person in the coffin face?) can be pursued in writing. Write about wedding processes; *If You Want to Marry a Zulu* (or Sothos, Xhosa, Shona, etc.) could be an intriguing title. This also applies to *Genealogy of Tribal Fashions*, for instance.

You have a platform to share your life with others. Pass on the little stories and the art, music, and culture that is disappearing in the concrete jungles where we now live. There is no shame in our past. We can stand as a people in our skins and shields and pierced ears and tell a story. It is fake to listen to the snobs who say to forget history and let bygones be bygones, while others still commemorate the Holocaust and the battle of Sandwana.

As the people crossed the Red Sea and the River Jordan, God advised them to take stones and build monuments so that when the children ask what they are, they can be told, "It is Yahweh who brought us out. When the Jordan was surging, God stopped the river, and these stones are exhibits of our journey." Given a chance to write history, please write and preserve the faith. At our deaths, we can't leave behind the toxic waste of atomic reactors and plastics; let it be a legacy of knowledge, and such gruesome trials will not happen again. Embrace education, and let it liberate your mind. Read, and love knowledge; it's a shelter to the one who has it. It is a tool that can be used to gain materials.

Education without moral balance and ethics is the reproduction of small, clever devils. For every citizen of world—atheist or Christian, pagan or circumcised, barbarian or civilized, Catholic or Protestant, Muslim or Buddhist—there is a code that connects all of us to fair dealing. Leaders of today need a strong sense of distinguishing right from wrong, a desire to live right and enjoy favor with mankind in harmony with God. Further, they need the moral will to make choices. In the wars of the Middle East, the bone of contention is that they are fought from a wrong *moral* background. The morality of the war can't be verified. It is wrong to be at war because you want oil. You want to plunder another country of its resources, and then you maim the citizens, turning peaceful people into hostile ones, ultimately destabilizing the region. Do the Americans and the British have the *moral* right to be in Iraq? Judge for yourself.

In our global village, it is now critical to investigate things that bring us together, rather than those that divide us. Long before we are intoxicated with "isms," religious fanaticism, economic greed, and the pursuit of vanity, we are still people. We need food, water, shelter, and relationships that are meaningful.

It's a pity to look at our academic institutions, which are producing snobs and abstract graduates with flying colors. They graduate with honors but are bankrupt of interpretation, understanding, analysis, evaluation, and comprehension. This world is still lacking in thinkers who will push the boundaries of thoughts and formulate new principles. True education is not regurgitating the writings and research of masters. Making a personal contribution to your true profession improves the lives of people.

To make an impact, you must have a strong sense of morality. The difference between right and wrong must be crystal clear in your soul.

This separates criminals from wealthy people. True riches can't be made on the blood of others. It is evil to water your garden with the tears of your employees, neighbors, wife, and children. There are those who are married to their laptops and are flying high in their careers at the expense of their families. That money will be like gravel in their mouths, and the sniffling of their children will never be a blessing. Again, I advocate for a balance between these areas of life.

"What is written in the law, and how do you read?" Find out what is in the law, and interpret it so that will communicate the truth to your spirit. It is appealing to gather to yourself those who say what you want to hear but will not build you. Better is a little salt to the wounds, for then they will heal.

"What is the law?" The moral law (the Decalogue) is the best guideline across the board.

For these section headings, I am quoting the Bible, New Revised Standard Version as follows:

1. I am the Lord your God, who brought you out of the land of Egypt …

This commandment establishes belief in the existence of God, in his creation, and in a demonstration of the power to deliver people from bondage to freedom. The Old Testament law is a document promising passage from slavery to the promised land. You have freedom because you live in compliance with the rule of law of Jesus.

True liberation is to walk away from the Egypt of coercion and tyranny, toward freedom in Jesus, to love God with all my heart, then do as I please. God is a pillar by night and a cloud by day, and I am truly liberated, even walking in the wilderness amid food shortages, snakes, and heat. There is a difference between the pain of a slave and the pain of a free man. Immanuel is not a New Testament promise but an Old Testament companion. How do you read? What is in the law? The law says you are free.

Still stuck on what he must do, the lawyer is reminded that Yahweh has already finished. Why start doing? Instead it's a celebration of the historical acts of God.

2. You shall have no other gods before me. You shall not make for yourself an idol ...

Your total allegiance is to God alone. It is prohibited to worship additional gods, spirits, or incarnations. These deities have hands but can't touch; they have ears but can't hear; they have eyes but can't see; and they have legs but can't walk. The entire book of the Torah strongly condemns humans for kneeling and worshiping things that are smaller than God.

Never bow before the gods of other men, whether they are success, money, looks, or achievements. In worshiping and bowing before these things, you twice humiliate yourself. You are admitting that you are smaller than the idol and twice as small as the maker of the idol. Do you dare to reduce yourself to being the grandson of an inert, indolent, and torpid sculpture?

Human beings created in the image of God can't reduce their importance and sink into the meaningless veneration of lifeless fakes. You will be like whatever you worship; worshipers are never bigger than their gods. What is written in the law? How do you read? Your genesis is divine, and your destiny is with your creator.

The discussion is not about what I can do, but the fact of what is written. The law is written, and God is legally bound to save all who believe. The sinner will do his best, and God promises to do the rest. Claim the promises, and keep your obligations, for God is firm in his vows. I choose to worship God and let my ways find meaning in him.

3. You shall not make wrongful use of the name of the Lord your God ...

The law forbids lies and cheap oaths. God is never pleased by the worship of idiots. Placing the name of God next to mischief and professing that God is your witness is treason. It is written in the law that God will do whatever he promises.

The lawyer came and addressed him, saying, "Master, what must I do?" It seems that the lawyer was accusing God of not being clear on the terms of entrance into his promised kingdom. When Jesus looked at him, he referred him to the law. In simple terms, don't play with God. He is not your high school buddy. Approach him with holy fear. He is the genesis of all that is, was, and will be. The lawyer was made to remember that God does not lie.

The command is clear and simple: don't use the name of the Lord for evil purposes. All candidates for the kingdom have access to the name, and the *use* of that name must be constantly in harmony with the principles of its owner, Yahweh.

4. Remember the Sabbath day, and keep it holy. For six days you shall labor and do all your work. But the seventh day is a Sabbath to the Lord your God; you shall not do any work ...

If the lawyer was listening to what the master was saying, by this point, he was defeated. The fourth commandment calls him to remembrance. He could only remember what he had forgotten. This one is a reminder of a few principles, including the Sabbath day. The rest day celebrates the completion of Yahweh's creation, when he sits in satisfaction over a completed task. This law is a majestic rest, and all men and women are invited to take part. This is the first verse in the Bible that teaches righteousness by faith. The rest is an invitation, not because you have worked, but because Yahweh has finished. Even if your duties are still calling, Sabbath (rest) and *shalom* (have peace with God).

This is a health command that takes away all stress and anxiety, a true challenge to the lawyer's argument. "What must I do?" There is nothing much left but to accept the invitation to enter into this rest. Masters dwell in an empire of tranquility. Masters must find time to rest, regain their strength, and clear their thinking. The Sabbath is a day to revisit the beginnings, swing into the very presence of Yahweh, and refuel, collecting gems of wisdom in preparation for the challenges of the coming week.

Every professional needs to get this principle right: to have enough energy, tap into the reservoir of the divine. Plug into the main station of holy current, and let your apparatus function empowered by truthful law, justice, and mercy.

Truly, the Sabbath observance is not for slaves and servants. The Bible puts it in perspective in these key words:

- *Thy work:* Right there, God addresses self-employment; do your work, not their work.
- *Thy servants:* God assumes that you will be a master with a work force and servants in your household, not one, but many. The master's house must be full of visitors. Masters need big tables to entertain people and introduce them to their secrets of power.
- *Thy gates:* God assumes that you will have a big house with many gates, not one gate.

Not all qualify to go to church on Sabbath, only those who meet these requirements. Worship is best if it is the praise of masters, with a testimony of how the Lord has blessed them during the week. It is on this basis that to refuse to work with God at your station of labour is dreary and tiresome. It deprives the saints to receive blessings at the Alter.

5. Honor your father and your mother …

The extension from Yahweh's relationship to community and others is very clear. Whatever you have learned from Yahweh, do it to others. This obligation extends to parents and the way masters should manage these relationships. For lack of understanding, people talk about rights and the equality of men and women as a new thing. The Bible says that God created them male and female; honor your father and mother. The two aspects are put on the same level.

Arguments can be listed that state that equality doesn't mean sameness. A sexist would struggle to ensure preferential treatment for one sex. The maker made them equal. "Parents" here means elders. Understand that you are born of the same species and society that masters dwell in, passing respect from one generation to the other.

The measure of respect that you give to your elders will directly come back to you. In giving, you will also receive. The acts of mercy are cyclical. "What goes around comes around." In the law, it is written that unless you have a clear understanding of relationships and have mastered the dynamics and management of them, it will be a challenge to inherit the kingdom. It's a social kingdom with no caste but family.

6. You shall not murder.

One day, I was given words of wisdom by Maponga Joshua I. Having completed graduate school with good grades as a qualified theologian, I was summoned for an interview by my grandfather. The questions were simple and to the point, but the process was very slow and intentional. At first, I received showers of compliments for successfully going through my learning without bringing the tribe any shame. "Well done! What did you learn in your six years at the seminary?" In response, I listed the things I had studied in my first year: Christian beliefs, communication skills, aerobics, psychology, physiology, philosophical biology, arguments of metaphysics, epistemology, core subjects in Old and New Testament theology, Greek, ethics, and marriage dynamics. He was listening very keenly as I bombarded him with big terms while struggling to translate them into our language.

After my long lecture, he posed the next question: "What does the Old Testament say about the Ten Commandments?" I quickly paraphrased the commandments, explaining the horizontal and the vertical relationships, the Catholic view, the Jewish view, and the Protestant view. Quickly I framed the New Testament commandments as a summary of the Old Testament law.

His third question was difficult. "What does the sixth commandment say?"

In my simplicity and incomprehension, I blurted out, "Thou shalt not kill."

He interjected, "I know that. What does it mean?"

"Well," I suggested, "The Torah teaches us to be cautious of the sins of omission and commission. A murder can be intentional, and in defense, one can also commit this sin. Jesus addresses intentions and motives of the heart, saying that it is tantamount to murder to wish someone dead. A nod of approval for someone to point a gun and shoot a person is tantamount to attempted homicide."

My grandfather, Maponga Joshua I, looked me straight in the eyes and said, "The Bible teaches 'Thou shalt not kill.' What you have said is book knowledge. Whatever the Lord has given you, thou shalt not kill. The profession that you have chosen, thou shalt not kill." With these remarks, the interview came to an end. I was ordered to go and get some water.

Years later, I have learned that my grandfather, who had not even a primary school certificate, was a stream flowing with wisdom. It has taken me years to realize the wealth and the beauty of such a revelation. I must not kill emotions, relationships, truth, influence, integrity, initiatives … the list goes on. Life is a connected honeycomb. There is a hub on which everything is hitched and sustained.

The lawyer was being taught that masters are not criminals, murderers, swindlers, or midnight gamblers. The master should not be found with blood on his hands—the blood of business colleagues, family, or community—either by commission or omission. Those who have made themselves into sharks will be eaten by fellow sharks, in the same way that those who kill by the sword will die by the sword.

Those who run kingdoms and administer empires can't gang up over the carcasses of fellow humans and rejoice in their demise. Build up others, and rejoice in their success. It is written in the law: don't kill people, even in your thoughts. At times, you will hear yourself say, "I don't want anything to do with him. As far as I am concerned, he doesn't exist."

Masters are those who have become champions and tamers of the difficult. They are riders of wild horses. They catch snakes by their tails, and these turn into walking sticks. They touch swelling seas and make pathways between the separated waters. They can drop a leaf into a pool of poisonous water, and it becomes a fountain of sweet water. Masters talk to Yahweh and command the bakery of heaven as chefs in glory, preparing breakfast for the pilgrims. They reduce the flying distance of quails so that they may be caught by hand.

True masters have learned how to master situations. Their presences in the deserts turn the dry and weary land into wetlands. Best of all, masters can touch rocks, and they become springs and flowing rivers, bursting with life, hope, and possibilities. You are a master; you shall not kill. Let them look and live. Lead them through this wilderness. At the sunset of your days, point to the promised land ahead and tell them you will not cross with them; bow your head and die, and they will mourn for forty days.

How readest thou? (Luke 10:26)

The commandment "You shall not murder" is a summary of the last four remaining commandments.

7. You shall not commit adultery.

In committing adultery, you kill commitment and trust. You kill the marriage, and you kill your conscience by doing this evil. Those who have made sin entertainment would dance "where angels fear to tread." This road seems right at the beginning, but its results are ways of death and absolute devastation. Children are forever confused and grow without a correct perspective on life. Single parents hire nannies and struggle to balance the training of their children and not lose sight of their personal lives that are social and intimate. Endless court cases turn lovers into plaintiffs and the accused. Adultery is murder. It leaves the two parties permanently damaged and paralyzed. In some cases, even suicide and murder are considered during this torment.

8. You shall not steal.

When you steal, you kill the other person and deprive them of the use of their goods; you will have killed happiness. The person who has lost his property is pushed to the verge of murder. His spirit is crushed, and his trust in fellow humans is killed. Stealing is killing. Masters don't steal, for it is killing, and the reward for killing is to be killed later.

9. You shall not bear false witness against your neighbor.

When you bear false witness against your neighbor, you will have killed his reputation. The lives of other people sometimes end up in your hands. A comment that you pass could make them see the light of the day or turn them into breakfast for the dogs. Many children, careers, and marriages have died in the hands of unwitting criminals. The words spoken have butchered and crushed the soul. When optimism is lost, people give up trying. False witness is murder, and masters don't kill.

10. You shall not covet your neighbor's horse ...

In the building of your empire, personalize it with a distinct stamp. To covet other people's things kills personal initiative. It kills creativity and bears ill feelings and jealousy. In the journey to obtain goods, prestige, and wealth, masters don't covet their neighbors' donkeys. A mean-spirited person will not be happy to see a rival prosper; in many instances, there will be a desire to see rivals fail, and in some cases, there will be a wish for their funerals.

*   *   *

After all Ten Commandments were cited, read, and understood, to answer the last question ("How do you read?"), the lawyer went on to summarize the book of the law: "You shall love the Lord your God with all your heart, and with all your soul, and with all your strength, and with all your mind; and your neighbor as yourself."

Three relationships come to light: the love for God, the love for neighbor, and the love for self. Mathematically, the ratio is 4:1:1; love God with all your mind, heart, strength, and soul, then love your neighbor as yourself. You must love God four times more than neighbor and self. When the conduit of life is directly perpendicular to God, a horizontal axis with my neighbor will produce a right angle where I meet God and my neighbor meets me. It is impossible to be right with God and have a crooked perception of the rest of his creatures.

A marriage situation is portrayed by the triangle below:

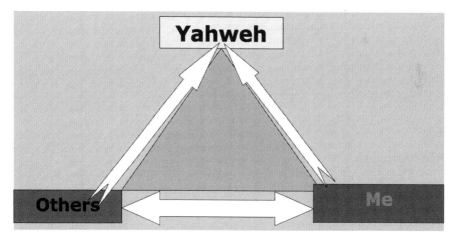

Fig 3.1. Maponga J

The distance between me and others will never be covered. There will not be a day when I will fully understand my wife or those around me, but there is a miracle in the triangle if both parties start on a journey to move upward, find higher goals, and seek God. In short, as the two parties are moving up from different directions, they are getting closer to each other. Yahweh, at the apex of the triangle, draws the two opposites to a common destination. So yes, in him, they are one. It's painful exercise to try to please partners and everybody else that can't please themselves, but it can be made easy when both parties make an agreement to meet at the top. In a similar vein, organizations will do well when they establish a common objective, so that the entire organization can aim toward the apex. Some people move from company to company, and wherever they go, the company closes. The problem could be that they isolate the company vision and mission from the foot soldiers. A tea boy or janitor can bring business into the company if they are fully made to understand the business principles.

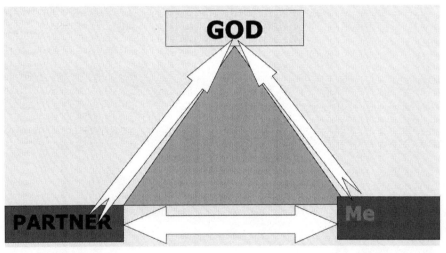

Fig 3.2 Maponga J

Profitable businesses are smart to use POISE. Hugh Davidson, in his book *Even More Offensive Marketing,* describes the principle of POISE:

- **P**rofitability: A proper balance must be struck between the company's needs for profit and the customer's need for value.

- **O**ffensive: Let the organization take the lead in the market, take risks, and make competitors follow. This is being the brand leader.

- **I**ntegrated: The marketing approach must permeate the whole company.

- **S**trategic: Probing analysis lead to a winning strategy.

- **E**ffective: Strong and disciplined implementation should happen on a daily basis.

Let me add D to make it *POISED*

- **D**ovetail: Meet customers and keep them. Dovetail clients and service providers, and know who to call and when so as to foster strategic partnership. The integration reaches every facet of the company. Whether it is a family, a church, or a company, this principle of dovetailing or rather networking is relevant. Until those who are on the journey with you see what you see and hear what you hear, you might be moving ahead or walking alone. Successful masters will initiate dialogue. Also, they will keep the focus on the core business.

Reflections

Here are four things to reflect upon as you grow as a master. Find out how you do these things:

- Reflect on what has been spoken
- Verify with the written word
- Identify the "moral of the story"
- Interpret and apply accordingly

In the Bible, read Exodus, chapter 20, and reflect upon it.

Applications

- Start writing a journal, a story, a song, a poem, a book—anything. Please write!

- Preserve memories for future generations.

- Develop a strong sense of morals, and let your decisions be founded on this moral solid ground.

He said unto him, what is written in the law and how readest thou?
(Luke 10:26)

A master must be guided by the idea of preservation of the purity of life; no life will die in your hands, mind, or heart; the law will be the template that orders life. Masters will constantly move upward. In finding God, they find everybody else. They amalgamate culture and transcend the borders of the hoi polloi. The triumph is that after they find their spiritual anchor they will find themselves and find others as meaningful partners. For a master to live is to share self with the community.

CHAPTER FOUR

MASTER OF ACTION

Thou has answered right: this do and you shall live.
(Luke 10:28)

The devil is a liar, saying God's requirements are impossible. The devil says, "God can't be pleased. It is impossible to keep the law. No one is perfect, and no one will ever reach the requirements that God demands. All marriages have problems, and no one is happy." We turn on each other at times of crisis, when all our dirty laundry is aired. After we have finished calling each other names, we turn to our children. Frustrated by all these "impossibilities," we push the trouble and stress onto our children. "You can never get anything right." "You are so stupid!" "How many times must I tell you the same thing?" "Are you deaf?" These types of phrases come out in the open, driven by emotional trouble.

To reach the full circle, we go to work, and all hell breaks loose. Emotional trouble accompanied by thorny words from a superior become the plight of the day. "Just do your job. If you don't like it, quit." "If you can't shape up, ship out!" "I pay you to do your work, and that is all we have in common: service and delivery." "We all have troubles. You have problems, I have responsibilities." It is clear that these aggravations follow us out of our houses and mess up many other good things in our lives.

When you can't get something right, anxiety develops. Some people will not be able to sleep. Children will scream and throw tantrums when they know they must get it right but it is wrong. You hardly feel good when you see a bad result. Students have committed suicide over bad grades. Company executives have hanged themselves over missed targets and seemingly unrecoverable deficits.

There is something that happens inside the human body that collapses the channels of clear thinking when failure is constant and defeat is obvious. It is clear that "cowards die many times before they die." Those who endure the night should share the secret of their endurance.

When we read of the lawyer who spoke to Jesus that night, we learn something of great value. When someone gets it right, it affirms positive behavior. Jesus is clear on the issue of affirmation and the building of human ego. When people gives you access to their minds and words must be spoken, let that be the most important of all times. Like sowing seeds in the fields of thought, the words spoken will grow and give fruit. Be proud of your gardens inside other people's minds. Idle words and cheap discourse is not fruitful. Let your talk be salted: painful at the time of delivery, but at the end, it heals open wounds. Let your lips be a salt shaker that seasons the diet of human deficiency, preserving the easily corruptible.

Just as salt heals others, it needs to heal you too. The words you speak to yourself are as powerful, and they may build you up or ruin you. Two types of self-talk go through our minds: positive self-talk and negative self-talk.

Positive Self-Talk

When you get it right, tell yourself, *That is like me.* If you see someone who is doing things right, please say something nice. Human beings always perform better in a happy environment. Be it church, company, or home, the occupants of these venues must be careful how they handle this critical and essential human emotion. If you want someone to perform a task, let them know that you have their welfare at heart, and you will surely get more out of them. Time, talent, and treasure can be sacrificed if it is appreciated. The juice that gets the extra mile is affirmation. It is sad to note that in some cases, incentives are big but affirmation is scarce, and the result is selfishness, not generosity. Human beings need to operate on a higher level than just fulfilling basic human needs such as food and shelter.

A master must work on pride. If a task has passed through a master's hand, it must be signed and sealed with a guarantee slip. A master goes to work to change circumstances, and whatever hands he finds to do a task, it is done with all one's might. Ultimately, this is how you can tell who will forever be an employee and who will be an employer.

Masters don't get threatened by excellent and perfect performance from students and fellow masters. Life is not competitive; it is complementary. Partners, colleagues, and spouses must look at each other and see their shortfalls fulfilled in other people's strength, so that when you are weak, they will be strong for you. How best can any company build a team? Unless this principle is understood, divisions and antagonism will break good goals, and brilliant strategies will gather dust on the shelves. Genius children will be turned into mediocre performers.

Masters produce masters. Here is a tool you can use to shape people, tapping into their creativity and patting them on the shoulder. "Well done!" "This looks excellent!" "I appreciate your support." "Given the chance, I would marry you again." Let those who are near you hear these words constantly. Praise gets into their systems and demands that they perform better next time. In animal training, they call it positive reinforcement. There is no director, chief financial officer, or chief executive officer who is immune to compliments. To create an environment conducive to compliment sharing at work, talk positively.

Masters must be careful to choose their entertainment carefully, as this will influence and inform their brains. Cheap games and immoral entertainment must not be the food of the soul. Let the master guard jealously the passageway that lead to the soul. Don't allow yourself to eat or drink with sinners and scoffers and be a contributor of evil talk. Delight in the Lord, and meditate on his word day and night. You will be like a tree planted beside plentiful waters, yielding fruit throughout the year. Place yourself on fertile ground. Periodically be where grace can find you. Take it from Jesus: "You have answered right."

Negative Self-Talk

"I can never get it right!" "I am stupid." "I am ugly." This type of venom cripples the human body and benumbs the brain. Slowly but surely, the human system begins to accept these negative suggestions. In the process, feelings are altered, and positive goals are clouded. A drive for excellence is substituted with average postures. Ultimately, performance will start to dwindle and agree with the mind. It's one thing to bury a dead person, but a negative person is twice as heavy. That is why the grass grows very tall on their graves. God forbid that grass should grow on my grave.

Negative self-talk can be communicated at all levels. In life, you will find others who have nothing in their vocabulary but negativity. It can be communicated verbally or nonverbally. A master needs to have enough tools to cope with both means of communication. Start with yourself, and meet the world. Your attitude permeates your immediate environment, sending signals to those who are near you to influence them for good or bad. There are some people you want to avoid because of how you feel after you have been with them.

The company of negative people kills initiatives and destroys dreams. At times, there is a need to learn the power of privacy. A seed goes into the ground and hides from everything. In the right moisture and temperature, it must die and reappear as a plant. There is power in incubating good ideas against dream killers. There are those who believe "it can't be done." Airplanes, software, and other technologies are here to prove that it can be done, against all odds. Pessimism is the fuel of the unfaithful. It is therefore not advisable to share your dreams with the dream killers.

When you get it wrong, tell yourself, *This is not like me.* Program your brain for merit all the time. Reaffirm the positive spirit. Let failure and averageness not be the standard by which you measure your performance. If it doesn't make you happy, it will not make many other people happy. Even students must be marked not on the basis of right and wrong, but according to their extra effort, to push the wall of averageness back. A brilliant student can't be happy to get everything right when it did not demand effort.

Jesus said that if a man forces you to go with him one mile, go two miles. When the expectation is for one page, you strive to complete two pages. Great achievers have masters that the blessing found in the second mile. The expectation is to fill the requirement, but the second page is for character. This works on them and leaves you richer, wiser, tolerant, and more mature.

Human rights are an enemy of the gospel. A nation can't be built on selfish protection of these rights; it must be built upon a selfless offering of using good to destroy evil. Wrong habits must be uprooted at once. Let the master feel uncomfortable in failure resulting from poor choices.

Negative self-talk is cancerous and dries up the bones. It turns pleasurable duties into boring, mechanical functions. People trapped in negative attitudes knock their heads on walls all the time. A father must have pleasure in being a father, assume the responsibility with pride, and fulfill the duties required of a father. Mothers need to look at their tasks not as duty but pleasure.

Young men and women need to have another look at labor. Cleaning the house you sleep in is not a request; it's a demand of health. Cleaning plates that you eat from is not work, but life. Cooking food that you will eat is not a tedious duty; fasting is an option. This responsibility must be accepted and understood; it benefits yourself and then others.

Often people will want to argue about what they don't know, ignoring the future and unknown while ignoring the present. Jesus didn't base his answers on the unknown; he addressed himself to the readily available. "You have answered right. Go and do likewise, and you will live." All of us have an amount of right and wrong that we know. If you do the right thing, it results in life; doing the wrong thing results in death.

Jesus sent the lawyer home, saying to "do likewise." This means that these things must be practiced in the home, in church, and in the workplace. Theology informs us that where much is given, much is required, and where little is given, little is required. This presents God as being full of mercy, for with every truth, there is accountability. Those who live with the law will be judged by the law, and those without the law will be judged without the law. Go *and* do likewise, *and* you will live. There is a special conjunction given to us here: "and." Knowledge put together with *doing* results in life: doing and living. Life can be extended. You might have lived, but know that if you take the interior and make it exterior, you are in harmony. Life must be lived and be full of action.

This conjunction is preceded by the command to love. To do all and not to love is to die alive. All might be lost. If I have loved, I will have lived. Jesus tells the lawyer to *do* and to *live*. Lonely are the lives that people choose. Some lock themselves out of reach in solo, miserable self-penance. A real master walks and eats and does many things with other people, including crying. In loving, we place our actions in the hearts of others, thus challenging them to become like us.

Masters will live to be remembered; forever they are immortalized in the bones of their disciples. Even if you should burn them like martyrs at the stake and pour their ashes into the river, they will continue to live in the plants and people who drink the water. Let CEOs, ministers, mothers, fathers, and presidents alike leave behind an inheritance imperishable, that which seeks to elevate and enhance character and the buoyancy of the human spirit.

Scriptures tell us of acts. The book of Acts has not yet been finished. In terms of its writing, the complete version is in heaven when *your acts* are put side by side with the acts of Jesus, Paul, Elijah, John, etc. Every day we go out to write this book, but the world might not see it. We are writing for eternity. When you are given a chance to do, heaven wants you to immortalize your acts. In the books of eternity, these will be forever on record.

Masters don't die. They live in every park; they are written on every wall. Libraries tell from shelf to shelf that they were here; machinery, gadgets, inventions, songs, footprints on the moon, satellites in orbit, multinational corporate companies, and folktales live to tell their tales. To "do likewise" is to live for eternity while living in the present.

Reflections

- Do you try to do things right? When a relationship has gone bad, do you initiate reconciliation, or are you apathetic about it?
- How do you relate to your partner, workmate, associate, wife, or husband?
- If you are the boss, how do you rate the style and language you use with your juniors? What language do you use to get things done?

Applications

- Make a commitment today to try to be polite and effective without being abusive. Rid your mouth of vulgar language.
- Talk to yourself well. Affirm positive behavior, and rebuke negative tendencies.
- Pass compliments truthfully, and openly admire good things; it improves relationships.
- Avoid violent and impure entertainment; it soils your spirit. Don't make filth your amusement.
- Avoid negative friends while you are building your self-esteem.
- Do some intelligent tasks, and derive pleasure in doing them yourself.
- Write your own affirmations, and remember:
  - You are a blessing, a gift to the community,
  - People around you are sent by God. The people given to you as family and associates need your careful attention and support.
  - Do your level best to live right and be a positive source of light.

You have answered correctly; do this and you will live.
(Luke 10:28)

As a master, you must refuse to die. Refrain from acts of death; instead, let your acts be permanent; they are the ultimate affirmation. Let your actions be in support of life. Go and do likewise, and you will live in harmony and tranquility.

Chapter Five

Master of Self-Esteem

But wishing to justify himself... (Luke 10:29)

Seeking to justify himself, he asked, "Who is my neighbor?"

- Who is my neighbor?
- Who lives next door to me?
- To whom am I related?
- Who shares a wall with me?
- Who is the person I must nurture?
- Whose welfare must be of concern to me?
- What is the criterion of help?
- Who deserves my love and care?
- Where and with whom must I spend my concern?

All the questions raised are good, but the motive of self-justification is wrong. Self-justification produces excuses for our behavior and highlights our unwillingness to overcome weakness when our character reveals a discrepancy between theology and practice. It is the reaction we project when our sins are uncovered (Genesis 3:10–13). Our lawyer comes out as similar to a son of Adam and Eve and portrays the same cover-up techniques when he seeks to justify himself.

When our sins are uncovered, what is our first reaction? Is it common to man? Refer to Genesis 3:10–13 and Ecclesiastes 7:16. Being overzealous about your righteousness and wisdom can end up destroying you. It blinds you and makes you fail to grab the opportunity of correction and repentance. You will grow only as you repent and admit that you are wrong. Sin and weakness can't be covered up. Pleading temporary insanity is not the solution to a sickness of the human heart. The question of the lawyer goes on to show the human problem and the three evil spirits that eat our souls.

We need to consider two complexes and one result that drive self-justification: superiority, inferiority, and low self-esteem. This is the bank of lies, excuses, and underperformance.

A superiority complex is an exaggerated feeling of being superior to others. It is a psychological defense mechanism in which feelings of superiority conceal feelings of inferiority. On the other side, we have the inferiority complex. This is a condition or a disease of the human spirit. It is a subconscious neurotic mechanism of compensation developed by the individual as a result of unrecognized feelings and feeling unloved. Those who attended universities will remember that Psychology 101, a first-year class, outlines the inferiority complex as a cluster of repressed fears for which the sufferer will overcompensate by developing a superiority complex.

Behaviors related to these mechanisms may include an exaggeratedly positive or negative opinion of one's worth and abilities, unrealistically high or low expectations in goals and achievements for oneself and others, emptiness, extravagant style in clothing (with intention of drawing notice), pride, sentimentalism and exaltation, snobbishness, a tendency to discredit others' opinions, forcefulness aimed at dominating those considered as weaker or less important, credulity, and bad attitudes when rebuked or confronted with situations that demand change.

Low self-esteem lies at the core and can wreck the human spirit of drive while constantly trashing opportunities of repair and correction. Seeking to justify oneself is a destructive habit that says, "I am right, and I have good reasons for why I did it that way."

In *Managing Your Mind*, Gillian Butler and Tony Hope list the signs of low self-esteem, paraphrased below (I have amplified some issues):

- Feelings of being unloved, always looking for love

- Overdependence, inability to make decisions, always consulting

- Extreme jealousy and overprotectiveness

- Excessive worry and anxiety about trivialities

- Fear of trying new activities (risk-taking)

- Perfectionism: some will surround themselves with an abundance of nice things, thinking this will overcome the constant feeling of insecurity, but the accumulation of material things will not provide a sense of genuine well-being.

- Inability to describe or even understand feelings

- Frustration

- Excessive anger and irritable behavior

- Need to overachieve to prove to others and win their confidence

- Poor school or work performance

- Being highly critical of self and others, never impressed, and hard to please. A constant tendency to boast of one's abilities—even to the point of lying about achievements—is a red flag. "Let another man praise you, and not from your own mouth" (Proverbs 27:2).

- Continuously being in poor health and constant signs of pathological disorders

- Poor posture, slumping, and lack of self-love

- Inability to look people in the eyes, fear that they might see through you and see your soul

- Sexual promiscuity. Many young people starving for affection—hugs from their parents—surrender themselves, without reservation, with anyone who is there to provide a warm hug and an understanding heart. What is true for a youngster is the case for many adults as well. A lack of personal esteem is a prime cause of sexual immorality.

- Drug abuse. Self-deprecation has driven some to immerse their woes in alcohol, hard drugs, or a daily pill-popping routine. Drugs are so deceptive. They promise much but deliver nothing—except carnage. Drug abuse is one of the major problems of our nation. Much of it stems from a self-perceived lack of worth and a sense of purposelessness regarding human existence.
- Eating disorders
- Self-mutilation

A master needs to find the cause of these complexes and unpack that pain so as to turn weakness into strength. Bear in mind that the most prominent cause of low self-esteem is an involvement in personal sin. It is what we do to ourselves. Sin scars terribly, and some damages will last a lifetime.

Observe that the world of philosophy and secular psychology has utterly nothing to offer the person of low self-esteem. The ideology of unbelief can't generate any true and lasting sense of personal dignity. True answers to the human emptiness are found at the manufacturer's yard—by going back to God, who said, "Let us make man in our own image." Our content and appearance are by the design of the chief human architect, which is God himself. Yes, sin has marred that true nature, but you can't allow your inner person to be as evil at the world outside is.

"Seeking to justify himself" is trying to prove a point while not being willing to lose the limelight. Further, it is trying to safeguard one's skin, afraid of being proved to be wrong and ill-bred. Trying to be right, finding reasons, and trying to be smart is defensive. Weak human characters can't tolerate exposure. The educated lawyer discovered that his arguments did not hold water at all, and it was clear that he had been a fool to ask questions when he already had their answers.

Those who ask the wrong questions always get wrong answers. Some married people operate by guessing and making prophetic predictions. They never tell you that they miss you, but instead send lots of nonverbal and verbal communication that ends up as mixed messages. This is tantamount to misleading a partner, for it is not easy to read someone's mind. Life would be easy if people clearly declared their needs and made it easy for everybody to help.

Who is just? Who is right? The lawyer came another time and said, "Good master …" The reply was that no one is good except the father in heaven. Expectation of righteousness in a reality where no one is good turns all craving for goodness meaningless. Human beings must not expect too much from each other. It is always amazing to see people expect things from others that they have failed to realize in their own lives. A wicked man feels comfortable marrying a Christian woman to compensate for the shortfall; it's religion by osmosis, or salvation by association. In so doing, they hope to receive God's favor in the shadow of their praying partners.

Justification can't be found in this search, but only at the point of encounter. A sinner or drunkard hears the voice of Jesus calling, "Is there a sinner out there in need of a savior?" At the moment when they say yes to the divine call, God clears their slate of evil, and they are made right with God. Justification is a divine act when God reconciles his wrath with a willing sinner who accepts the plan of salvation. Again, it is not in what we do, it is what God does. It is possible to be made right with God.

To be justified, the lawyer needs to learn that you can't do it for yourself. God does it for us, by expiation. Either God does it outside of himself or within himself, but all is resolved in the heart of God: whoever believes in Jesus will be saved. Accepting the invitation of grace and realizing humanity's lack is the prerequisite of justification. Cheap religions miss the point by teaching members "how to justify themselves" rather than having God justify the sinner. If we had the capacity to help ourselves by "actions, penance, pilgrimages, and chastisement," there would be no need for a savior.

"Seeking to justify himself …" Many sinners think that they will put their hearts right before they come to Jesus, but this is a fallacy. If you are able to fix yourself, then why come to Jesus? Come as you are, and let the cleaning up be a joint venture with the master.

"Who is my neighbor?" The profound question exposes the lawyer. When he should be the one telling Jesus, he decided to ask the question, "Who is my neighbor?" The struggle in his life exposed him as clearly dissonant. That is seeking to appear right and trying to justify wrong decisions.

There is a new word in the dictionary: "animality." It doesn't have its bad reputation for nothing. There are miseries that automatically follow sexual infidelity, murder, impulsive aggression, and child molestation. The great capitalist sings these three verses: "Show me the money," "Mind your own business," and "I don't care." All behavior is justified as procedures for continued existence. For example, smoking is an inverted gratification; it is an objective injury that is understood as a gratification. Other examples are cosmetic self-mutilation and religious flagellation. Here is where we begin to understand the extent to which the human search for gratification unfolds in the mind, the monumental extent to which it is a matter of interpretation.

Smokers began to blame their suppliers for causing them to smoke and thus to pay the suppliers to kill them. A smoker who defiantly continues to smoke after knowing it is harmful has transferred all of the responsibility to the suppliers and has justification as to why he smokes. Similar are a driver caught in a speed trap, a husband found in the wrong bed, money moved to a wrong account, and a word spoken at the wrong time. Why do people find reasons to condone iniquity?

The orchestra of justification is never a solo work, but a duet, and "so we walk together, my Lord and I." There is a cure for low self-esteem. A master should thrive for excellence and regain lost dignity by plugging into the main power supply. Self-esteem can be regained when a master finds his knees and knows that it is God who justifies the sinner.

Here are some extracts, for your growth, from Desmond Morris's *The Naked Ape: A Zoologist's Study of the Human Animal.*

Causes of Low Self-Esteem

These are known sources of low self-esteem. Let us consider the following factors:

Physical Features

Do you feel unattractive in your physical features? What is your viewpoint? Are you overweight, or too thin, or ugly, or do you have crooked teeth, for instance? Remember, while physical characteristics may make an initial impression upon others, they are subordinated rapidly to personality qualities. Some who are quite attractive physically are so obnoxious in disposition that folks are loath to be around them. Others who are a bit "plainer" have tons of friends, because intelligent people are attracted to their charm, wit, compassion, or overall spiritual depth.

Lack of Education

Do you feel low self-esteem due to a limited formal education? Remember this:

Some of the wisest and most prominent people of history were not privileged with an abundance of formal schooling. King Sobuza, King Moshweshe, King Shaka, Abraham Lincoln, and Princess Magogo, among others, may not have seen the doors of classrooms but were wise and brilliant leaders and military strategists.

Some of the stupidest folks of history have been laden with education. The expression "educated fool" did not arise in a vacuum.

It is never too late to learn. Some have acquired college diplomas and university degrees in their sunset years. On the news recently, a woman over eighty years old graduated. When asked about her future, she said, "It looks very bright."

Tragic Circumstances

Did a tragic event happen in the past, one that you feel is holding you down? Low self-esteem may result from tragic circumstances in one's past. Abortion is one example. Or a person may have been conceived out of wedlock or as the result of rape or incest (where your grandfather is your dad too) and so harbor self-disgust. Children frequently suffer from low self-esteem because of the vile deeds of their parents. You need to learn that you are not responsible for the wicked actions of others. Self-reproach is unwarranted in such cases.

How do you think you will progress when, as a father, you know there is a child out there with whom you have nothing to do? Make things right. Pay maintenance, and reconcile your life.

Physical or Emotional Abuse

Abuse can ravage one's self-esteem. Frequently, a parent or spouse will berate a child or a companion persistently and viciously, so that the victim's sense of personal worth fluctuates. An uncaring husband may tell his wife that she is ugly, fat, stupid, or lazy. Using words to torture people can be as devastating as physical brutality. Some children's psyches are damaged enormously by sexual abuse. Constant harsh criticism also can wound a youngster's sense of personal pride.

Victims of abuse must learn that they can get past these horrible experiences and find true happiness in living. You can be the master even of your own emotions, and you can work past these experiences.

Sin

One of the most prominent causes of low self-esteem is involvement in personal sin. Sin scars terribly. It is sometimes the case that one who loves God deeply and who strives for spiritual maturity will, in a moment of weakness, fall into some dreadful form of wickedness. The crushing blow of such a transgression may have lasting effects that so debilitate the person that he or she has a very difficult time regaining a sense of Christian dignity, particularly if others have been privy to the transgression (read Psalms 32:3–5).

Yielding to evil can rob the conscience of that sense of well-being God intended us to have. But there is a remedy for sin that allows one the opportunity to recapture his sense of joy and purpose. Get rid of sin in your life. Isolate yourself from schemes and plots of evil, clean up your act, and prepare for a life of power.

Reflections

- Rate your reaction when caught doing the wrong thing.

- Have you ever thought, *Who can make me right?*

- Do you need supernatural help? Do you need God in your life?

- Why do you try so hard to boost your self-esteem? Do you have a problem with the success of others, or do you have esteem deficiency?

Applications

Self-justification may have its roots in low self-esteem. Here are some of the areas a master should visit to find out if there are bones in the closet. The following application may be painful, but hey, you need to start somewhere. Go on and squeeze the boil; that's how it heals.

But wishing to justify himself ... (Luke 10:29)

Seeking to justify himself, he asked "Who is my neighbor?"

CHAPTER SIX

MASTER OF SYMPATHY

A certain man went down from Jerusalem to Jericho ... (Luke 10:30)

The reality is that life is full of surprises. All strategies and plans put together will never equip a person for life. Education and simulations prove to be insufficient for all eventualities. Prayer, fasting, and pastoral gimmicks don't always give the expected answers when reality questions our intent and actions. It is possible to work hard and still fail. It is also possible to study and burn the midnight oil but still have low grades.

Marriage can sell you a pig in a bag, like Jacob waking up the following morning to discover he had spent the night with Leah. A curriculum vitae (CV) can be a collection of false representations of a person on paper, and the person you hire may not be like what his CV portrays. The job you applied for and the one you are doing now might be miles apart.

Here is the secret of masters:

Adaptability

Related words are flexibility, elasticity, litheness, nimbleness, adroitness, agility, and dexterity. This cluster of words defines practical application, consistence in the midst of change, and dependability cushioned by survival instincts.

It doesn't always pay to cry when you feel like you have been short-changed. Look at one master, Joseph. He was born of his father's favorite wife, Rachel, the girl of Jacob's dreams. By right, Joseph was the first-born of Jacob's choice, and Jacob could not hold back his love and affinity for his real son. Jacob's other sons were born of Leah. These were painful reminders and the fruit of the scams of Laban. Jacob could not restrain himself; he made a jacket of many colors for Joseph, to the rage of Joseph's brothers.

You can't be loved by all. Even those that God loves might be hated by their brothers. For instance, Joseph was visited by God in dreams and visions. When God blesses a man, there is little the world can do to build or destroy. The revelation of God and the love from his father, Jacob, gave Joseph an advantage over all his brothers.

When you have done nothing wrong except to tell your brothers about your dream and put on your jacket, jealousy breeds envy, and destruction is the result. In the dungeon sanctioned for a crime he did not commit, he should have asked, "Why?" Sold to traders en route to Egypt, in the shadow of his homeland, he should have wondered why. If there was ever a man who was shortchanged, it was him. Almost raped by a woman (sexual harassment), he ended up in prison, despite his innocence. Erring on the side of right, he refused to comply with sin, and for that, he was sentenced. There is no university, church, group, or guru that prepares people for such times.

Here Is a Master

In whatever Joseph did, he needed no supervision, and while in prison, he was given accolades. He was successful. How can one be successful while in chains and behind bars? Success is not the goods in your store-room or the balance in your account. True success is measured by who is on your side. When God stands behind you, you are successful. God blessed Joseph in all that he put his hands on, and he was put in charge of other prisoners. He made the best out of the worst situation.

We are all on our way down in this race of life. As a certain man went down, so are we all on a journey that has hidden accidents. The greatest disappointment is self-deception: to think that what happens to other people will never happen to you. Changes of environment and situation are rarely anticipated; if coupled with pressure and penalties, change can render an intelligent, spiritual, and upright man a lawless and senseless brute. God has to work hard not to allow temptations beyond our control to befall us; otherwise we all might end up lower than we think.

The only time you can laugh at death is when you are dead. Stop laughing at other people's scars, and use your privilege as the measure of the rule. Look at your hand: your fingers and the lines on your palms are unique. A master is one who has learned how to master his misfortune, turning it into fortune.

Be faithful to the task at hand. Don't mess up the present opportunity for ambitious stars in the sky. Financial miracles, jackpots, and lotteries are not things on which to build a life and a future. Build your wealth steadily; walk the ground only once to avoid recurrence and cyclical inanity. Some people are ensnared in error, like fools walking in a maze; doors that lead to success are ignored when egos the size of mountains are fed to no satisfaction.

Joseph mastered his brothers and their inferiority complexes. His vision was on the pinnacle of glory. God could talk to him and give him visions. He mastered service to bring supplies to his brothers in need. He always wore his jacket with pride; he mastered the dungeon, survived the slave traders, and conquered manual labor with precision and diligence. Also, he mastered his emotions and was in control of the inclination to satisfy the flesh at the expense of virtue and dignity.

Masters have emotional balance. While the world promotes self-expression, fantasies of eroticism become the diet on the silver screen. But they no more belong on the screen than they do in our actions. To move the libido from these private chambers would render a master into a sex beast, no more than a thoughtless animal.

So you want to be a master? Watch out for the road that leads downward. "A certain man went down from Jerusalem to Jericho ..." (Luke 10:30).

Figuratively speaking, Jerusalem becomes the high place. That is when you are in control and in charge, when you are on high ground, when right and wrong are clear, and Zion, the temple of praise, is within view. When parental guidance hovers over your choices and your accountability is on surveillance, it is easy to live right. When mentors are holding your hand and you can bounce your ideas off of them to minimize risk, it seems easy. Once the downward movement commences, disaster looms in the air.

These are moments when you can see sanity leave a man and irrational, erratic, acerbic tendencies set in. A man leaves his five-bedroom house, Jacuzzi, and waterbed to have a sexual fling under a bridge. A man sacrifices the safety of the *mkuku* (tin house) to fulfill urges that run on the loose, with unimaginable repercussions. This also applies to women. This road leads to death. It's the playfield for those who lack discretion, and knowledge is dragged along as a soundless partner. While looking at the seeming beauty and honey that flows from lips of folly, their rational thinking is hypnotized, only to wake up with lamentation and irreparable scars.

So you want to be a master? Avoid crooked and hot deals. Shun those who speak to you with their eyes. Don't go near the entrances of the house of temptation. Be mindful that you will spend your money and strength building other people's houses, while your future languishes. Drink water from Jerusalem, and feast on the water from your own cistern, according to Proverbs 5:15. Bless your fountains with presence. Let your partner rejoice with you; spend your time making memories that will grace your golden years. A prostitute will reduce you to a loaf of bread (Proverbs 6:26). Masters on this road of the simple-minded don't lack judgment and loiter on the streets at twilight. They are super-careful.

Masters will not use sensual favors for promotion and appraisal. Those who are baptized in these licentious waters are spendthrifts, moving objects of mistrust—now here, now in the street, then on the square. First they say, "I love you," and then "I said I loved you, but I lied." Smooth talk never buys honesty. Those who live following rhymes and flattery, like an ox led to the slaughter, will die a slow death thinking it was going to be better.

Masters walk on the same streets, hand in glove with their lifelong partners, for they are married to wisdom and dressed with understanding. Masters are never available for rented partial fulfillment. Seasonal pleasure can destroy long-term goals. As with Jacob and Esau, a mess of pottage can buy a birthright. People will approach a swindler to seek what they have lost, but even with tears in their eyes, they will not find it.

The way that leads away from Jerusalem goes into the outskirts of protection and place the dupe into risk, with no guarantee for tomorrow. The journey between the two cites, Jerusalem and Jericho, can't be taken unwittingly, for it demands vigilant pedestrians.

One wrong business decision, one wrong marital decision, or one wrong social decision can utterly destroy years of exertion and reputation. Masters can lose some things, but for others, the price tag is too dear a sacrifice. Character, honor, and sound moral judgment must never be impugned by bribes. The voice of conscience leads a master, so that in losing, there is gain. A master needs to understand that sometimes in gaining, there are losses. History records the fast beginners and slow enders.

A certain man went down from Jerusalem to Jericho ...
(Luke 10:30)

Make your honest business Jerusalem. Make your happy home Jerusalem. Make your community Jerusalem.

Stop looking for greener pastures when you are standing on brown grass. Maybe you need to be a master and learn the effects of water on brown grass. How about mastering agriculture, which teaches you to water your garden so that others can envy you and refer to your turf as the greener pasture? Stop jumping from job to job in search of these pastures. Make your present company pay the revenues that you deserve, and devise methods to reward your employees. Before you go down, talk to the master who turns wildernesses into green pastures.

The employee you want to fire might be the best thing for your company if he is well placed and his skills are directed to the right task. As farmers grow crops, masters grow people.

Stop changing partners and rushing for divorce papers. It is all the same; tame your beast with goodness. Turn the desert into a fountain, and plant an oasis of hope within a barren land. Stop to think about the rubbish you want to throw away; there are a dozen people who can't wait to jump into bed with them. Jumping from the frying pan to the fire could be the result. So you want to be a master? The wealth you are looking for is in the mouth of the fish you have caught. Masters will throw their nets at an instruction of faith, repeat the same task, and get better results with the right attitude. Cast your nets to the right, with personal effort, and there will be more catch at dawn than at night. Do the right thing again.

You can only kill evil with good. Real success should be measured by the ability to manage and lead our homes with truth. The frustration that we feel in failing to handle our home affairs always makes its way into the boardroom. Frustration at home messes up our sense of judgment and renders us insensitive and impatient bosses and colleagues. Masters manufacture happiness and distribute it freely and abundantly to the family, and the surplus to workers and communities.

Stop changing communities, looking for houses in the suburbs, where the elite hide their misery behind tall walls. A dog in a corral will never be a cow. Your presence in that suburb could actually mess up the good vibe. A master doesn't look for a place; people look for the master. Elisha in Dothan would instruct army generals to go and bathe, without even looking at them, because Naaman had come in need of help, despite his reputation and posture.

It doesn't matter where you are. Be the master and awaken change. Plant trees and golf courses, open saunas and steam rooms where you are. Franchise gyms, fast food outlets, and boutiques turn the neglected, despondent masses into a hopeful nation.

Masters make places. In Soweto, there is a small house that has little furniture, but because a master lived there, Nelson Mandela, the prisoner-turned-president of South Africa, trips are organized from Europe, Asia, and the States and elsewhere to come into this match-box and smell, touch, see, and rub shoulders with history to arouse our moral obligation. Here is a bed where the master was sleeping. Prison cells have been changed into tourist attractions because masters spent years in them. Relics and artifacts become priceless because they were in the hand of a master.

Masters come into places, and they change the very names of the places. Of course, people rename those places with history in mind. You are no longer Jacob, but Israel. You are no longer Abram, but Abraham. He named the place Bethel, and the city is build four square. Its name is the New Jerusalem, for the old things have passed away. *Behold, I make everything anew.* No more tears, graves, troubles and sorrows, pain or dying. The grand master, the great I Am, in whom all things are, with him we are; without him, we are not. He has shown us that his presence paralyzes evil and displays the hidden. Look again; when he is done, it is better than it used to be, and traces of the old can't be seen.

Reflections

- Reflect on the lives of those you think are strong. Read their stories, and uncover secrets of their success.
- How do you feel when you see others doing much with very few resources (for example, handicapped people, the mentally retarded, or the paralyzed), and you are doing so little with so many resources?
- It's important to ask where are you going. What is the fatal attraction on this Jericho road?
- In which direction are you leading your life?
- What are you leaving behind, and what do you hope to find?
- Can you see actions that lead you on the downward road?
- How do you make and manage your money?

Application

- Adapt to the changing environment without sacrificing principles.
- Stop evil before it occupies and destroy your soul. See it coming, and kill it.
- Don't take risks with evil.
- Stop now, and assess the direction of your life so far.
- Highlight your inclinations toward self-destructive behavior, and put corrective measures in place.
- Pinpoint areas where you have lost control, and map a way to gain mastery over those areas.
- Make up your mind to be a master.
- Constantly build stable investments, and make your business honest; it will yield returns and look after you.
- Make your home happy; you live there.
- Make your community a better place to live, and rejoice.
- Develop green pastures wherever you are.

A certain man went down from Jerusalem to Jericho … (Luke 10:30)

Before you go down, like all do, be a master. You can choose to be a casualty or a master on this highway of life. You can be the helper or the helped.

CHAPTER SEVEN

MASTER OF SITUATIONS

And by chance there came down a certain priest that way, and when he saw him he passed on the other side. (Luke 10:31)

At times, help is so close and yet so far. A married woman sleeps next to a husband whose interests are too far away, or a husband will miss a woman while sleeping next to his wife. These are the painful realities that happen in our lives. It's sad to make big blunders when those who can help are a call away. At times, we can even hear them walk past, like the man on the roadside. He heard the footsteps, but the Church father was in a hurry: too busy to help, and too preoccupied to lend a helping hand. So did the Levite walk on the other side? Religion doesn't help people, but Jesus does.

Orientation here poses a threat to human survival. The way the priest had been trained, the heresy he had come to accept as truth, hindered his ability to help. It is this wrong education and orientation that poses a threat to human life. In life, one should step in where there is a cry for help. Failing to do so, you are harboring a wrong education that will shorten the hands of its students and reduce the sight of its teachers. The world can't live with these academic cripples.

Until now, one would never understand the dangers of schooling. Yes, school produces some of the worst candidates of life. Schooling sometimes kills originality and innovation. Religiosity is but a form of godliness that does the worshippers no good. Companies need to be weaned off of meaningless formalities that hinder the effectiveness of its employees; bureaucracy can kill bright ideas.

These are the three books standing tall on my library shelf:

- *Gandhi's Passion,* Wolpert Stanley (2001)
- *Mandela,* Anthony Sampson (1999)
- *The Autobiography of Martin Luther King Jr.,* Clayborne Carson (1998)

The three countries that suffered under oppression from colonization needed saviors to redeem the dying souls. These three men stood shoulder to shoulder within one generation to shape the twenty-first century. One thing they share in common is that they all mastered fighting evil with good. Using violence will only make evil prosper. Retaliation is not a remedy, Gandhi warned (Wolpert, p. 243). It makes the original disease much worse. These three men addressed the "poverty of conscience." King asserted that existence is a raw material out of which all life must be created.

A productive and happy life is not something you find; it is something you make. When machines and computers, profit motives and property rights are considered more important than people, the giants of racism and extreme materialism are incapable of being conquered (Carson, pp. 231, 318, 340). Our system of government needs to approach the subject ecclesiastically rather than secularly; every nation and company need to grow and sensitize its "loyalty to mankind."

When a man is found lying by the roadside, those who are timid and fearful will always tiptoe past the man who needs help, worrying about their own safety. The famous will be asking if this is popular and will call for applause from the spectators, but those with conscience will ask, "Is it right?" Organizations need to take a position that self-safety, politics, and popularity should not be priorities, but simply obeying the voice of conscience that says it is right to do so is of paramount importance (Carson, p. 342) . Walking past those in pain can be a paradox in which we wonder "whether it is those inside jail or outside jail who suffer most" (Sampson, p. 311). How does a man or woman go to bed at night, having neglected a cry for help from a brother on the wayside? Where is the conscience?

Those who have made a difference have sacrificed their lives and forfeited their personal freedom and privileges for others. The priest and the Levite who walk past on the other side are the worst elements of society. How could they even call themselves religious leaders when they demonstrated such poverty of conscience? Having seen and heard the man cry, to walk away is tantamount to murder.

For a moment, we should consider the feelings and thoughts that went through the mind of this man as he saw the clergymen iron their professional regalia and profess to be rushing to meet God. Surely the god the priest worshiped was pushed farther from the reach of the wounded. Maybe the question should be rephrased: How clean is your god if he can't be soiled by the blood of the wounded?

F. E. Bleden, in his song *Hark the voice of Jesus is calling*, wrote these words:

> While the souls of man are dying
> And the master calls for you,
> Let none hear you idly saying,
> "There is nothing I can do!"
> Gladly take the task He gives you
> Let His work your pleasure be;
> Answer quickly when He calleth,
> "Here am I, O Lord, send me."

To wake up every morning and face another day is a privilege. There is a work to be done, a life to be touched, and a difference to be made. People can't just live and be alive and contribute nothing, pulling in oxygen without breathing out life into others. Within this great calling, the calling of life, each life must reach another, and this task is sufficient for every day.

When a master meets people at the greatest point of need, the master becomes their strength. While walking on this dangerous road, a master is aware and walks carefully, for he or she could be here but once. Opportunities are never to be ignored, and valuable tasks are not to be postponed for the morrow. If it should be done, it should be done today.

One factor that the priest and the Levite forgot is that the bleeding man got there before they did. The plight of this man easily could have been their fate. It could have been anybody. As I said earlier, people must not be helped based on culture, color, or creed, but for the simple fact that they are people. A neighbor could be anybody who has been bruised by the enemy or anybody in pain. It doesn't matter what color their skin is, what passport they have, or what accent they have. The human race needs to stand together and address the real adversaries: calamity, disease, poverty, oppression, segregation. Whoever causes pain to the human race is a devil to be exterminated. Policies that reduce human beings to slavery at the hands of lords can't be tolerated. Every voice should resist and challenge inhuman oppression.

Gone are the days when third-world countries were used as dumping sites for toxic waste. Like the man left on the roadside half dead, so is the condition of the third world. Young children share drinking water with pigs. Sewage pipes feed into the rivers among others. Sickness and epidemics are rampant; the forests are plundered for exotic wood.

I can't imagine parliamentarians drive passing the ghettos of Gugulethu and Khayelitsha to Parliament when the people along the road are perishing to nothingness. I can't imagine the oil pipes running through the fields of Nigeria, and on the other side of the pipe, people are languishing in absolute poverty. How do you explain the oil fields of Iraq and Angola, and the communities that are being given guns and funerals in exchange for their oil? Martin Luther King Jr. said, "A nation that continues year after year to spend more money on military defense rather than on programs of social upliftment is approaching spiritual death" (Carson, p. 341)

When those who can afford to help walk past those who are in tears, they are as guilty as those who have committed the crime. Puppet governments forced upon the third world by the economists of the West, in the name of democracy, are a disgrace. It is a known fact that democracy can be bought, and the so-called democratization is voted slavery that picks a few fat cats and put them in capitalistic positions to manage socialism. Budgets are drawn, but years into independence, there is little change in the lives of the people lying by the roadside. Why?

The pain is gruesome, bearing in mind that some of these people have been here for both of the two eras of apartheid and independence. Throughout African history, there is a monster that kills the sensitivity of the poor once in a position of power. New breeds of black masters assume the white whips to continue where the white man stopped. It is even more painful to be crucified and killed by your own kind.

When we see government officers and their signatures under our coats of arms, we think we will get help; but too often, the poor are left to die by the roadside. Where is sense or conscience? The tycoons, by world standards, are standing tall, with their ropes of honor hanging on their fat necks and lying on their chests and big tummies, yet they are morally bankrupt. Why does the black demonize his own black brother or sister? It is incomprehensible. This is the paradox of life envisaged by wise Solomon, the philosopher of old.

A clarion call is made here in this chapter: Political parties need to read this story and after understanding, write their mission statements. The same applies to governments. Politics have made some societies unthinkable and uninhabitable. Fights and gruesome killings continue to threaten the communities. It is sad to note that the opposition leaders continue to drink coffee in Melrose Arch, while the communities they are said to represent are swimming in blood. Political parties need to define themselves as breakdown services on this highway. Rescue the bleeding. Democracy should be used as a means to an end, for people, not as a destination of social politics.

Until these groups can give a clear message of how they are going to address themselves to social ills, they are not ready for power. This can be done without going to Parliament. Let the parties stop campaigning, but instead dig trenches and build houses for the poor and galvanize support from true service. Talk is cheap, and its value is nothing if is not accompanied by action. We need to walk the talk and not to talk the walk. Governments need to wage an aggressive onslaught against poverty. Our parliamentarians should stage a "courageous confrontation of evil by the power of love" (Carson, p. 25).

Reflections

- Looking at your life—physical, mental, social, and spiritual—which area is a source of pain or stress?
- How much damage have you caused by using violence, and what course of action can you implement to make a difference?
- How do you derive pleasure from the pain of others? In short, how do you feel when enjoying riches that were stolen from the hands of the poor?
- Access normality, and seek help where possible.
- Find out who is your neighbor.

Applications

- Identify a student or junior you can coach.
- Be a friend of the green world. Plant a tree or some grass. Be part of conservation.
- Visit the ghettos or slums, and have a look at life in the poor communities. Devise a plan that will make you a source of strength.

And by chance there came down a certain priest that way, and when he saw him, he passed on the other side. (Luke 10:31)

The abundance of evil has made good actions abnormal, and people no longer act well out of the natural world. The life of a master is wired by sensitive cords that are moved by the pain of others. As life presents various situations to you, it demands your actions. Nothing happens to you with no reason. Whatever your hands find to do, do it with all your might.

Chapter Eight

Master of Service

But a Samaritan, who was on a journey, came upon him; and when he saw him, he felt compassion, and came to him and bandaged up his wounds, pouring oil and wine on them; and he put him on his own beast, and brought him to an inn and took care of him. (Luke 10:33–35)

This is how to be a master:

1. **Walk the same road the common people walk.** Experience can't be infused by remote control. Going through a situation gives you firsthand information that will assist in decision making.

2. **Be where they are.** Don't stop until you are shoulder to shoulder with those in your community, family, or relationship.

3. **See them, and listen to their cry.** Don't judge a situation, as you might miss the point. Listening is more important than talking. God gave us two ears and one mouth, so that we might listen more and speak less, where possible.

4. **Get off of your donkey.** It might sound a bit uncomfortable, but you can't access the situation from your donkey. You will need to deliberately get off of your donkey to reach the people in need. In short, move away from your comfort zone to where the trouble is.

5. **Touch them.** Reaching out to people with your hands is best. The way you use your hands can heal or destroy. Let your hands be cushions of comfort in times of pain and tears.

6. **Identify the wounds.** A good master will meet the wounded at their point of need. Don't waste medicine; apply the remedy to the problem with exactitude.

7. **Oil the wounds.** Masters do not fuel hatred, and they don't increase discord. To oil the wound is to control infection, allowing the process of healing to begin.

8. **Bandage the wounds.** Protect the wounds from external elements, and let healing take place in a safe environment.

9. **Lift them up.** Lifting people from where they are to where they should be is the right motive.

10. **Place them on your donkey.** Volunteer to walk while the patient rides your donkey.

11. **You have to walk today.** This is power that places the welfare of others above one's own comfort.

12. **Find an inn.** It is a place of help. Take care of them all night long, pay the fee, and make promises that you can keep. "I go, but I will come back and pay for any extras."

The good news is here. You are not alone at the hour of trial. Yes, pain will be felt. It confirms that you are human. Those who walk past also show the weakness of the human spirit. Don't lose your faith in the human spirit. Masters are still around. They might not ride Crossfires, Ferraris, Cayenas, E55 Mercs, BMWs, Rolls-Royces, or other top-of-the-line vehicles. There is a master riding on a donkey. It is not in complexities but in service that we can identify a good master. Flamboyancy and titles within the temple circles had not converted these men to be leaders and masters. They were worse than criminals, yet surrounded by glory and false humility.

The master or the Samaritan was on his way too, walking on common ground. As they had walked, he was walking in the same direction. Know that there is nothing new under the sun. The fingerprints you leave can only be yours, even in years to come, and no one else's. A certain Samaritan, seemingly unrecognized and despised, marginalized and excluded, came along.

Let us move the story to our century, where life is characterized by these things:

- Xenophobia
- Nepotism
- Dangerous ways of life
- False hopes
- Gender inequity
- Cross-cultural diversity
- Filling in the gaps

When those who are supposed to be on the job are not there to do it, these things occur:

- Crisis management
- Medical services
- Empathy for human pain
- Things that render people half-dead
- The use of oil in healing wounds
- Carrying each other
- Caring for each other
- Sacrifices
- Walking while patients are riding
- Well-positioned social services

- Night vigils
- Cash flow
- Paying bills

People and organizations need to find a spiritual reason for social responsibility. Why people do things is more important than how they do them. At a spiritual level, common gestures of service are transformed into worship. The doer stops being accountable to the receiver, becoming accountable to his deity. Social responsibility is a religious ceremony that professionals need to be comfortable with. It is on this altar that the sacrifice of service needs to be offered and sustained.

Labor on its own is a spiritual activity that is in obedience with the word. The duties one performs at a place of work need to have more value than remuneration. Every job we do should be in service to mankind. Through our work, God is blessing people. We are channels of resources to better lives, environments, and families. Negligence at this level is equivalent to societal genocide. To refuse to carry responsibility or to do it without care shows ignorance of the impact of responsibility.

As you do things, do them as unto the Lord. "If you do it unto the least of these my brethren, you do it unto me." The manner in which you and your organization treat people is informed by the spiritual reservoir and the foundation of your company. Let every company find its spirituality, for where people meet people, it's a spiritual encounter. Those who make it have discovered that it is fruitless to divide people into groups. Human life and experience is holistic. When a person stands in front of you, it's not a coincidence or a physical, mental, or spiritual encounter; you have met the total being. The best impact can be made if we use the entire spectrum of appeal to trigger the right response.

It is sad when companies are expected to be more interested in money than in people's welfare. The customer of today has moved from being a gadget collector to a service seeker. People want service and after-care for the products you offer them.

In corporate strategizing, great care must be taken to find this spiritual connection that will shape the vision and mission of the organization. Some corporations and their associates have resorted to fancy, lifeless statements of intent that highlight their desire to dominate the industry rather than measure their ethos at the point of contact with society. I find such slogans bankrupt of spirituality and relevance.

The business world now has new multinational, capitalistic, and monopolistic giants. Asia and Africa have a lot to teach these multinationals; people are more important than business. Yes, the law says that the business of business is business. But on the soil of these continents, the business of business is people. The love for people and improvement of the social fiber must be at the core. The accumulation of fat bank balances is short-lived if the people who contribute to their growth are raped of the benefits of that growth. Find people to make money, and find money to help people to improve, and then your money reserves will improve too.

Here is another idea worth considering. If the business of the church, for example, is to collect money and help the poor, then what is the church doing to improve the giver so that the church can collect more? The quantity collected is equivalent to the possessions of the giver. If they had more, they might give more. How on earth can the church think that a business is secular, when secular business sponsors religion with tithes and offerings? The fields in which the congregants work in order to bring their offerings must interest the church. The church needs to position itself as a partner in corporate development, for it is here that it will prosper. The promotion of a church member is parallel and comparable to the promotion of the church.

On the same level, it is important for an organization to be interested in the capacity of a worker to deliver the required service. Home and social issues are important variables in an employee's performance. Roads, networks, family, security, water, spirituality, sanitation, infrastructure—all play a part to deliver a worker on time, with a smile, ready to be productive. If the business is aware of social ills that ruin the performance of the employees, it is equally important to address these ills, for as a worker is happy, so does his productivity increase. All things are connected. This spiritual connection needs to be cultivated, maintained, and sustained.

The source of the offering must be developed for the fulfillment of the mandate. You can't milk a stone or constantly harvest where you never sow. Development must begin to grow into social corporate ethics, like the woman who found her lost coin. Let corporate stories be told about changed lives rather than monetary targets achieved. Products and services must be constantly evaluated, based on what people are saying about them. Synergies must be found for individual and corporate relevance.

The passage simply states that the Samaritan "came to where the man was"; he met him at the busy road. How good are we when we run past the finish line and continue to run? When you pass people, the race is finished; you can't continue to run and leave the people behind. You can't be a miracle worker or healer who walks past a hospital to perform miracles in the stadium. How practical is your faith if it causes you to walk past beggars and the lame in town while going to a tent revival? If Christ were walking with you, he would stop, go to where they are, and say, "Get up, pick up your bed, and go home." It's time we question hyped, charismatic pseudo-Christianity that only works when there is an organ playing and an offering plate full of money. It's also time to question cheap theology that teaches that God will bless us as we bless him, thus placing God and man in competition. God is God, even without us. Also, God is powerful within us.

When corporations and individuals find a spiritual reason for doing good, the platform is much higher and we are assured of diligence and monetary remuneration. The posture of worship makes sure that the quality of work is supervised by the *unseen*. It is not a crime to build a culture of worship at work. Executives need to stop acting like gods. They should attribute success where it belongs. Aligning employees to a higher spiritual platform will help them to overcome their personal problems and usher them into a divine realm where excellence is of paramount importance. Employers must stop being afraid of religion, for consumers are religious, and so are employees. If workers associate their work with evil, minimum output will be realized. Build your company in harmony with God. Employers, let your workers feel and know that God is also at work and that their duties are extensions of grace, to reach and touch others.

Education is learning and unlearning. The two processes must be run concurrently in the formal or informal classroom. The tradition that teaches people cleanliness and defilement loses its soul when it fails to hear the human cry. Programs and holiness in venues becomes obstructions of service. When people begin to behave like the priest and the Levite, society will die in their presence. How can you walk away with the excuse that God will not accept you with the bloodstains of a brother? This religious ceremony clearly shows a nation rotten from the top down. If you see a person limping, the problem is not the leg but the head, which has lost concentration, allowing the leg to be hit. If the custodians of mercy fail to care for people, the common people can only do worse.

Education that doesn't teach people human service and claims to sensitize the human spiritual inclinations, cultivate the voice of conscience, and tolerate interruptions is altogether useless. Forms of religiosity can destroy the people and the clergy. If I can speak in the tongue of angels and pray to chase demons ten miles away without love for people, such ceremonies are meaningless, and they render me a gonging cymbal.

The love for God and the love for others must precede and supersede the love for self. Only after understanding this principle can we realize that selfish love is destructive. Programs that rush to meet God, leaving people in anguish, are an abomination to the author and finisher of our faith. If you can't see God in pain in the life of your neighbor, you can't see God in smiles in your life. The letter of the law must be escorted by the spirit of the law, lest we become mechanical robots. Policies that govern structures and bylaws that protect our investments should be enforced by the letter and the spirit, or we will turn our homes and offices into police stations and dungeons. Note that there is blood beneath the dry flesh you are dealing with, so tread softly, with tender care.

Teach the people to go down. Teach the people depth, not heights. People's motivation must not be how high they can go but how deeply they can reach people. No one is in the clouds where we push performance. People are on the ground.

Here is a story. A pastor from the seminary came with four degrees to a parish of the semiliterate. It was rumored that as he unfolded his discourse, all the people would look up to the sky, waiting for him to come down. He would float in the stratosphere of theological jargons and touch the cumulus clouds with syntax, etymology, and grammar, and not come down. He slept one night and dreamed of himself walking the very clouds where he dwelt. While he walked in the clouds, God shouted for him without showing his face. For a long time, before the pastor got offended by the calling, he told God, "If you want to see me, show your face, and let's talk."

God answered, "I am down here with my people, on business."

It is painful to realize that diminutive and negligible service at our doors, if done with precision, will make God happier than the sacrifice of a thousand bulls. God will not hear the prayers of a man or woman who is at war with his or her partner. For when God comes down, we must go further down, to humanity. Jesus came all the way from heaven; we only have to kneel down, and that is the depth of our service to each other and to God.

A father kneels to mend the broken toy of his child. A wife kneels to pick up a husband who has failed his vows. A community kneels down to assist the family to bring up its offspring. A boss kneels down to evaluate and support the one who could not meet the targets. A church kneels down to cry with the bereaved.

Life is service. This is what God did for us. We can't do less than uplift the fallen. Many churches and corporations don't understand the powerful ceremony of the Lord's Supper. The idea of washing each other's feet is the only guarantee we have that assures us that no one eats with dirty feet and there is no soil in our food.

Customer service and relations between companies can be improved if the dish-and-towel concept can be understood and practiced. Wash the feet of your client. Yes, the business is eating, but wash their feet first. Better still, it is the responsibility of the home owner to make sure that all guests who enter the house have been washed. If you have read this far, you need to find that towel, and carry the dish to the doors of those you have wronged, and begin to make things right. If you are in an office, make a difference today. Take your lowest employee for lunch, and bounce some business ideas off him.

Let social institutions and corporations place a dish and towel at the door, so that the tycoon can wash the feet of the door keeper. This is unlearning hierarchical worship for service. Again it must be said: go down where the wounded are. Reach out to the gutter. Be a master who is moved by the pain of others, and do something about it. Real masters do not move into communities with trucks full of gifts; they walk the dusty streets with a broom, a towel, and a dish of warm water to relieve the sweat and pain of the downtrodden. Masters make it their duty to walk "the road less traveled," with priceless service. Masters would rather use their hands than pay others to do things. Where is the morality in asking people to do what you can do or have pleasure in doing?

When you refuse to make that stand on the side of right, you have accepted death. You must ask questions of truth and justice in such situations. Cowards ask, "Is it safe?" The lazy ask, "Is it politically correct?" The vain come along and ask, "Is it popular?" But your conscience must always ask, "Is it right?" (Carson, p. 343).

Reflections

- Do you feel superior to all those around you?
- How difficult is it for you to stoop and help others?
- Does helping come out of you naturally, or you have to be coerced to do right?
- How do you feel when you are not recognized at functions, when you have actually made a sterling contribution?

- What is your organization doing to rescue and improve the employees bleeding and dying by the roadside?

Applications

So you want to be a master? Go down.

- Find a spiritual connection for every duty you perform.
- Motivate and inspire people to do things at a deeper level of spirituality
- Learn to unlearn backward traditions. Shun meaningless routines. Avoid becoming entrapped in petty issues, and stop majoring in minors.
- When confronted with a situation, place yourself into the shoes of the oppressed and disadvantaged.
- Find your dish and towel to wash people's feet. Don't entertain dusty and dirty guests before washing and making them clean first.

But a Samaritan, who was on a journey, came upon him; and when he saw him, he felt compassion, and came to him and bandaged up his wounds, pouring oil and wine on them; and he put him on his own beast, and brought him to an inn and took care of him.
(Luke 10:33–35)

Chapter Nine

Master of Joy

On the next day he took out two denarii and gave
them to the innkeeper and said, "Take care of him;
and whatever more you spend, when I return I will
repay you." (Luke 10:35)

A master must be free financially, as others are potential financial prisoners. Financial freedom accords masters the choice to liberate others into a powerful lifestyle, out of bankruptcy. By instinct, we all want to exercise power, command people, and make things happen. It is sad to say that the lion inside you might die in the cage unless you cut the lock and run on the land of economic independence. No one wants to go to work, for we were not born as slaves but masters.

Debt

These are robbers that carry tools to destroy your freedom. Masters need to have financial freedom. Masters needs to be aware of cunning thieves who cause harm, and rob people of their money, and harm households through crafty talk and sales. There is a malicious business trick: buy one, and get one free. This is pure marketing gimmick, making people dispose of their resources, and thus pushing the nation into impulsive buying. At the end, the nation goes down the drain: the bottomless pit of debt.

These shrewd marketers live in the present with no dream or vision, no tomorrow or plan for your life, only how to take more out of you.

They are thieves who live to plot and think about other people's wealth and how they can plunder it. They make long lists of who they can borrow money from and how they can catch the next victim. They ask for things without intending to bring them back; if they do, they arrive in bad condition. Theft is a lifestyle of the lazy.

On every busy road, a master is being warned of the devil, like debt is waiting to destroy the careless. It is naïve to assume that you are working with saints. Thieves don't only steal physical things; there is emotional theft, psychological theft, and intellectual robbery. Some have built their greatness on stolen property, and these are false masters. True masters give credit where it belongs.

A master must embrace his abilities and protect his assets. Poverty embraces the careless, who don't guard the mental properties that have been invested in their minds by the omnipotent. Charity and good will must not become a license for abuse. Every service rendered must be rightfully billed, and even when such services are donated, they must be quantified. There is a myth that when something is for free, it's cheap. Churches are guilty of abusing workers and always *wishing* people blessings instead of *giving* blessings.

Masters must exert themselves in the conduit of excellence and loathe sluggishness and the nurturing of indolence. To be found at the checkpoints of life in possession of stolen goods, with the actual intent of depriving the owners of the usage and of their commodities is treason to humankind. It is a shame to be rich when the owners of the ideas are poor and bask in lame excuses; these are ceaselessly heard in boardrooms: "Business is business." "It's a cruel world." "It's dog eat dog." You don't have to become one of the dogs and debase yourself, becoming odious and repugnant.

Customers

Debt kills joy and gives you guilt and a vexed spirit. Worry builds in the veins of customers. Be a master, not a victim of circumstance on the highway of life. Impulsive buying and accumulating debt is unwise. Demolish that bad attitude, so that it will not stand in the way of success. The simple idea is to identify your needs and wants and bank on long-term investments. Liabilities will make you a slave and leave you half dead, killing your libido and destroying your family and status.

Pay your bills, and live a debt-free life; don't buy more than you can pay for. Live within your means, and avoid credit. Don't dig deeper when you are already in a hole.

The Pharisee

These are the lazy fat cats who wait at the altar and collect offerings instead of working for their bread. The command to labor for six days also applies to the clergy. Faith without works is dead. Prayer must be combined with labor and dedication. Having done that, surely God will bless the work of your hands.

Every religious organization must be aware that its members are lying on the roadside, bleeding, and some are drowning and dying in debt. Walking past with an offering plate every Sunday will not heal the wound of debt. Masters who run these religious groups must transform the casualties into citizens of the kingdom who own land and servants. True worship must emanate from the threshold of praise, not begging. The reason to come to worship has to be giving thanks. "Let us come before His presence with thanksgiving" (Psalms 95:2).

Heads of departments and chief executive officers should develop debt alleviation schemes if they want to get more out of their employees. Organizations have employees who would have quit ages ago to have overcome debt, but they are still on duty, with little production. Why? The passion of some employees is not in their output, but in their monthly salaries, to pay their debtors.

New strategies and scorecards will not motivate these employees, for the more they make, the more they spend and the deeper they sink into debt. So you want to be a master? Here is an area you will need to look into: establish a good relationship with money. Don't make religion opium of laziness and think that prayer will accumulate wealth for you. Instead of spending money on luxuries, pay your bills and live a debt free life.

The Samaritan

This is the master. He or she is the one who travels with oil and can hear the cry in the woodland. This is what your life must be like, ever ready and equipped on the highway. No matter how rich you have become, if you can't help someone in trouble, you are still poor. Actually, it is sad to have help so close, and it leaves you in the same trouble.

True financial freedom liberates the master to spend and gives the master the heart to do humanitarian work, lifting those who are in less fortunate positions. The master has his donkey (transport), his wine (drink), his oil, his extra garment, and enough energy to walk while the patient is riding. A closer look at the Samaritan will disqualify many people we think are rich; in reality, they are poor. A master helps strangers and expects nothing in return.

*   *   *

Four milestone issues come out in this story, and they impact heavily on our finances:

- **Accidents:** Unforeseen eventualities. Life is unpredictable, full of ups and downs.
- **Health:** Don't use money to destroy your health.
- **Transport:** It could be a liability or a great asset. Treat it with caution.
- **Accommodation:** This is the sore part, as it must be paid in full and still leave you with a surplus.

Having a surplus is elaborated further, as follows:

Intellectual Resources

This is one of the most valuable resources, and it is one that many have not yet fully utilized. The human brain can be taught anything and can master it all. It is important for those who want to be masters to push the limits of fear and impossibility, to think, "Given time, I can." Broaden your horizons of research and reading, and build a storeroom of surplus knowledge. In many cases, this translates into common sense and constant adaptability to situations. Revisit those areas where you have failed and excelled, to see if you are still owing or need a top-up.

Emotional Intelligence and Resilience

Life will spend all the emotions that you have. Disappointment, black-mail, infidelity, rejection, or divorce might drain you and leave you empty. The master in you must have enough resources to love again, to hope again, and to trust again. The Samaritan says, "I go, and I will come back again and pay for any extra expenses." This appeals at all levels, and our emotions should be visited again for closure.

To be hurt and refuse to love again is to live in pain. Try again, like a toddler falling when learning to stand. Like a young athlete, run again. Like a student, do your corrections. Yes, you are wounded and maybe still bleeding, but hey, get up and make the best use of the life you still have.

To build these reserves, one needs to work with things that hurt to con-quer the emotional trouble. You need to expose yourself to people in a sim-ilar struggle and be of help. See how they deal with their pain. Find your pain too, and deal with it. A master can't carry the baggage of unresolved sentiments. These feelings will show up at a bad time and mess up the good character under construction.

Dip into your reserves, and find a reason to smile again and forgive those that have hurt you. Love those who hate you. No one will do this for you; just propose in your heart that you will let go and hug again. Have surplus emotions to travel again and assist others who are in need.

Physical Energy

The master must have tons of energy for the work at hand, and much more. Duty demands those who can go the extra mile. Always be pre-pared to do much more than what is required. This is how you separate yourself from the average. Here is a quick guide to help you establish enough physical resources for all seasons.

Living from hand to mouth is a reality many slaves experience. It is sad that the so many people will die in this jungle and never see financial autonomy. There must be enough for expenses and for a surplus.

The master says, "Here is the initial payment. I will come back and pay for any extra expenses." There was a blank check for the patient. His initial accommodation was paid for in full, and if there were other expenses, the Samaritan was coming to pay them. This is financial power. One can call it financial independence, which generates wealth.

Let masters come forward, demonstrate their power, and spend beyond restriction. They need to display the capacity to have equity beyond their monthly budgets. Every master needs a multiple streams of revenue, from consultation, commodity brokerage, manufacturing, manual labor ... the list is endless. In short, you need to put your effort into multiple ventures.

It is simple. If you have an idea, put together a business plan. Choose the correct timing, and establish it. Incubate the business at inception. Capacitate, employ, and monitor it. You should be free to do other things. Why toil and sweat in the mill and not teach someone to make money for you? Create employment for the "slaves" and those who are happy to work, and move into other ventures.

The master should be serving on a number of boards, constantly involved in policy issues and strategic decisions. Many people have businesses and think they are financially free, but these businesses are sources of stress and pain, because the people are bogged down in the mix of strategic and operational matters of their businesses. Get involved in the policy and strategic matters of your business, and leave operational matters in the hands of chief executive officers and chief operational officers.

I strongly condemn having one job or one business. In a nutshell, don't put all your eggs in one basket. You will soon lose out. It is uncalculated risk.

Spiritual Reservoirs

You need to find that connection with the supernatural. Be careful not to involve yourself with spirits that are lesser than the almighty God. I challenge you to plug into the divine. Mumble words into the air, and seek that supernatural intervention. Shout to the one you can't see, the one that you have heard occupies the skies and can live in your heart.

The challenge to you, the master, is to link up with the chief master, the creator of the universe. "Yet those who wait for the Lord will gain new strength; they will mount up with wings like eagles, they will run and not get tired, they will walk and not become weary" (Isaiah 40:31). Paying extra spiritual expenses is only possible when you walk and do not get tired, run and do not faint. Having surplus spiritual resources for others in need is a duty for the master.

Remember, you are running a breakdown service and making this world a better place to live. At every opportunity, give a helping hand. Reach out and touch somebody, and lift up their spirit. Your level of spirituality will permeate the places where you work and live. You presence will develop people, rebuke mischief, give hope, and encourage excellence.

The master is a shoulder to cry on during a spiritual crisis. They have germs of truth and understanding that make the present pain bearable. You want to be a master? Soak yourself in scriptures and the literature of truth, and build your first-aid kit so that you can help somebody by the wayside.

Reflections

- What is your relationship with money?
- Are you a master of finance or a slave of debt?
- Do you love yourself enough to free yourself from debt?
- How are you going to build your reserves?
- Do you have enough energy for the duties required of you?

Applications

- Puts systems in place to protect your mental, emotional, physical, and spiritual properties.

- Consider your spirituality to be the most important resource and source of motivation. Start today to build your appetite for spiritual things.

- Run a breakdown service, and have your equipment ready to assist those in need. Check your first-aid kit, and always carry extra oil and money, in case you meet someone in need.

- Start where you are. Touch your kid, your husband, or your wife. Be the master in your present situation, and grow that circle of influence.

- You are the master of the situation at hand. If this was the only time you had the privilege to make a difference, what would you do?

On the next day he took out two denarii and gave them to the innkeeper and said, "Take care of him; and whatever more you spend, when I return I will repay you." (Luke 10:35)

Chapter Ten

Master of Direction

All of us are changing, for good or for bad. As we meet situations in life, they either enhance our consciences or tear down the walls of humanity. If we are not on guard against evil, it has a way of reducing us to insensitive beasts. You were moved by the plight of people as a child, but now you can actually chase them from your doorstep.

Have you ever wondered what type of worshippers the levite and the priest were, after they left that man? Have you ever asked how they prayed, or perceived God? Did they ever think of the permanent damage they did to their consciences after they left that man bleeding by the wayside? They started to die inside their hearts. They would forever see that man in that condition and hear his cry. They extended that pain, built it into their system, and cast it into the shadow of their memories. Even long after the man was helped and eating corn, they continued to bear the pain.

When duty is demanded of you, to practice desertion or lack of care will do more harm than good to you. It will gradually collapse your internal walls of esteem and importance. The reality is that others are as important as you think you are. In reducing the value of others, you can be decreasing your value at an accelerated rate. Care and love for others automatically attach importance to self, and they help you to appraise your self-worth.

If you are struggling with a past that has taunted you, inhibiting convalescence, here is something you can do. To recuperate from these demons, first you will have to nurse others back to health. As they heal, you will reconcile with your pain and rebuild your broken spirit. Remember the dish-and-towel approach in the previous chapter. This approach works the best.

If you have been hurt by people in the past, it is best to be busy healing others, salvaging them from a similar situation. If you feel cold and find it hard to love, start loving and putting your arms around other people, and you will begin to enjoy their warmth. The vicious circle of evil must be dispelled before you can rebuild the virtuous circle of life. Counseling, with all its methods, will only heal in part, until the client decides to come face to face with his pain and conquer the past with the victories of the present.

The greatest pain is not felt by the man left on the roadside; it is felt by the one who walks away. He or she will never able to cross over that feeling of irresponsibility. After such gross acts of brutality, how did they look themselves in the mirror in the morning? To ignore others in pain will work to destroy ourselves. The Old Testament theology that advocates an eye for an eye and a tooth for a tooth will leave the nation toothless and blind. The few masters still walking on the streets must have enough faith in religion and love for people to change their present environment.

Learn fast. The value you place on others could be equivalent to your value. The respect and the support you give is what you may be getting in return. The rule is: "Do unto others as you wish others to do unto you."

Inhuman behavior destroys the fiber of society. Crime and vice are the products of a people who have forgotten others and lost their essence and tenderness. These small attributes are part of the animal kingdom, and the human race has a lot to learn about empathy and sympathy from these "lower" creatures.

Here follows an illustration of pragmatic thinking:

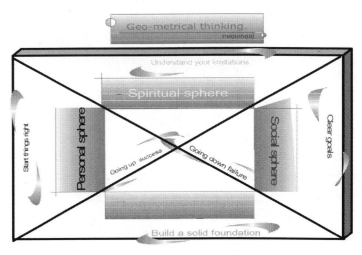

Fig 10.1Maponga J

There are four spheres and six lines, and God visits you at each line and sphere to give balanced, fulfilling support. Our decisions are usually based on one or more of these spheres and lines. You may ask yourself, "What will the church say? How does God look at me? What impact will this have on my social status? I wonder how my mother would react to this decision." You, the master, need to visit each sphere, walk on each line, and be familiar with your thought patterns and the sources that influence you.

Four Spheres

The personal sphere: This is your secret space. It is doing the things that matter to you and being selfish for the right reasons. You need to take time to go inside yourself, so that you can come out ready for others. Loving ourselves to love them is good self-love. Silence the voice of the masses and listening to what you want to do with yourself. You need to take charge and account for your actions, not basing them on what your church, family, and professionals think you should do. Find out what is in it for you. Also, you need to fulfill the desires of the inner self; when meaning is found at this level, it will make us endure and be impartial about principles. This secret space is a battlefield for dominion and decision making. The loudest voice writes law that governs the soul. Demonstrably, dealing with passion, earthly inclinations, and animal instincts is humanity.

The social sphere: Life is meaningful with interpersonal relationships. Even if you have billions of dollars in bank accounts, without people to spend it with, money has no value. Opening our arms to other people and exposing oneself to human pain and disappointments yields laughter and smiling with other people. Understand that as a matter of principle, you need other people, and paramount to your growth is a substantial premeditated interest. No man is an island, goes the maxim. In some businesses, the success of an entire deal will hinge on interpersonal relationships. It is important to understand how people feel around you and how you make them feel about you. Simple things like paying bills, recharging people's phones, or giving your airtime to make an important call will say more about you than a well-tabulated proposal. Little things counts in life, and it is a starting point for recuperation.

The professional sphere: With every skill acquired, let there be a drive to be professional. Common effort is not good enough. Masters should distinguish themselves with that touch of professionalism. It must be said again that every career must be mapped out, so that the direction of development is clear. It's sad to sit on a chair, knowing full well that you are sitting on the ceiling and you are not going anywhere.

Looking at broad-based black economic empowerment, many white males feel despondent about the new South Africa, and they are sitting on their laurels and crying for the good old days. Look for newer and better ways of doing things. On the other hand, some blacks are basking in the sun, claiming that the hard-earned democracy will automatically bring food to their tables on a silver platter. Plans need to be put in place. A clearly mapped direction for a master is of paramount importance; do not use your energy in fruitless experiments. A master should do everything possible, to the best of his or her ability, to produce the best practices and excellence, for the reward is exceedingly great and rich.

The spiritual sphere: This is the desire to interact with the outer sources of power, connecting with the paranormal to draw strength to deal with the normal. The soul yearns for supernatural power, wisdom, and longevity. The entire package is buried in deity. The type of god you believe in determines what his creatures are like. Within all of us is a desire to throw a stick on the ground and see it turn into a snake, and to touch snakes' tails and see them turn to wood again. Let every person be familiar with their spiritual tools, for the scuffle of life will require professional, social, spiritual, and mental fortitude. The spiritual component is crucial. Many times, when the common practice doesn't make sense, one need to engage in a higher level of consultancy and elevate meaning to a spiritual level. Without this to stand on, the human quest can be vicious to one's humanity.

Here is an illustration of pragmatic thinking, putting the six lines into perspective:

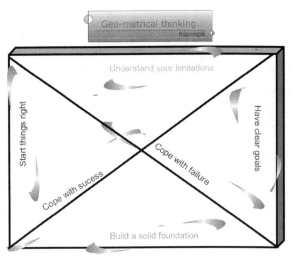

Fig 10.2: Maponga J

Here are six lines for equipping the master to make strides and headway in life:

One: Start things right. Every thing has a beginning and an end. Success is realized when the master knows where to start. Do the first things first, and the rest will follow. Calculate the cost, look at the options, and start at the beginning. In the profession of communication, we would advise you to start with the facts and figures (head), then proceed to the emotions (heart), then look at how people feel about it and whether they can make a decision and act on it (hand).

There is a flow of things that a master needs to know so that as to augment his efforts. If relationships are to last, they need to start right. Business partnerships usually give the most problems, because people don't start them right, and they join themselves with incompatible partners, to the detriment of a good initiative.

Marriages and careers will waste people's time unless they start right. These marriages and careers are bound to be expensive and will squander resources that are difficult to replenish. Take that trip to meet the parents and relatives. Do your preliminary research well; by the time you say, "I do," let it be based on the fact that you found rubbish in the closet and you are willing to live with it. Go through the initiation, and move to enjoy the privileges and rights that come with your present status.

Two: Understand your limitations. A fool will think that he is unlimited. This must not be viewed at a negative fact, but a master must identify areas of development after a thorough assessment of pitfalls. As we grow, our experience has some deficiencies that need to be topped up. Since God is in heaven and you are on Earth, truly there is a limit in that which leads us to his presence, unless he is involved. What is under his chair can be learned and conquered. On this level, the master must know where his skills end, so that others will add value. There are things that your students and employees know and can do better than you can. Understand your frailties. Observe the three-legged pot: the three legs all play a part to stabilize the pot, otherwise it falls and spills out its contents.

Many unwise people take more on than they are qualified to perform. Ultimately, they end up stresses and with poor outcomes, and they are seen as incompetent. This is misplacement of talents. Masters must avoid stress. They must not pile work on the desk of someone they don't know can deliver; otherwise, they are heading for failure. Yes, you must stretch your mind, but don't make it a core business. Years of experience will be spent in running pilot projects without completion.

Three: Set clear goals. Know where you will land and how you will arrive at that goal. It is sick to plant anger and hope to harvest love. Actions must go through a quality control center or a computer trail before they are carried out, so the final destination must be clear in mind. The error that many young people make is to think that the result will be different from the action. To travel on a train, not knowing where it will end, is a sheer waste of time. Before you board the train, please ask and verify its destination. Travel with hope, and you will arrive at your planned destination.

Four: Build solid foundations. Builders insist that a house is as strong as its foundation. A family will serve as the best foundation to start with. Establish strong family ties with your wife or husband, your children, or whomever is wherever you call home. Find a confidante, with whom there are no lies, and with whom you are truthful and share the darkest and deepest of secrets. Build these foundations strongest. Human beings are relationship-driven. We normalize in association, and so self-reliance can be detrimental at times. The saying that no man is an island holds water here. When good relationships are in place, they benefit the ones who maintain them. It is fulfilling to have a circle of reliable friends whom you care for, to nurture and add value to their lives.

Next to family is your spirituality and faith. Make sure this ground is solid, because during dark days, this is where you will find shelter. This includes your academic foundation, which will be good for employment and having a reputable knowledge base from which to run your life. Of importance also will be team platforms, where you fulfill the requirements of your role and colleagues are committed to your success as their success.

Five: Cope with success. A master must be able to know the steps needed to follow the upward road of success. This can't be left to chance. Fate will overtake the gambler. In reaching one's destiny and achieving goals, getting there might be a struggle, but living with success can be horrendous. Success can change people for good or bad. Waking up one morning to discover that you are better than your oppressors can humble you, or it can cloud you and veil common sense. Success, on its own, without a spiritual discipline, can become suicidal. Your internal braking system needs to be in excellent condition before you move over to the high-speed lane. A person needs to know where to stop and say, "It's enough."

You are only as strong as your weakest point. The building of people must be your occupation. Multiply yourself in your business. Transplant your goals to your team, and change your vision. Becoming their vision is one way of being successful and staying successful. To cope with success is to make others successful.

Six: Cope with failure. Going up is easy. Coming down is hard. It is a reality that all masters need to be familiar with the two roads: one that goes up and one that comes down. It brings a balance. This is not a quick-fix method, but that long route of permanent growth can set up a master to fail before he or she attains success. The concern is how to cope with that failure, to learn a lesson. Status, property, accounts, family, friends, suburbs, credit cards, insurance, medical coverage, overdrafts, school fees, membership cards, and credit rating—all these things cave in when you lose your job or when your company goes down the drain. In losing material things, the worst part is the noise that goes with it. The talking, the scandalizing, and the foul smell around you will all have an impact on your immediate circle. To deal with influence is difficult when you are always guessing that they might be talking about you.

In some cases, the comments passed on you are unfair, as they negate all the other efforts that you have made to get yourself where you are now. The wrong publicity will tarnish your image and cost you other prospects:

- Some will think that you were too proud.
- Some will think that you deserved it.
- Some will blame it on your poor skill and timing.
- Some will question your moral judgment and attribute your success to corruption.
- Some will be happy at your downfall, and others will be sad.

Not everyone can survive and learn to speak like Einstein, saying, "I have learned one method that doesn't work," or, like Ford, saying, "I will still build my company after going bankrupt a couple of times."

Steps to Follow

While you are working, put contingencies and insurance in place, in case you lose income. To have a long-standing insurance obligation counts. Understand the fine print when purchasing big items, just in case. Ask, "What happens if ___?"

A simple rule is to downsize your expenses. Use a smaller car, or return the big one to the garage or bank. Swallow your pride and use a taxi or ride a bicycle, if need be. Walk; you will be healthier.

When you are in a hole, stop digging. When in debt, stop creating more debts. When on the roadside, bleeding, stop cutting yourself in self-pity. It's bad enough what they did to you, but it's worse when you cause harm to yourself. Status is but a title. If you put too much of a price tag on it, it will cost you more than you can afford. You are what you are. Your true value must not be camouflaged by externally acquired goods.

Are you with or without substance? Define your substance; don't let your substance define you.

Learn from your mistakes. The only way to go down is to go down, close the leaking holes, and fix things. The wealthiest people have been bankrupt a few times. It is not going down that should matter; getting up is of the utmost importance.

*   *   *

In playing Snakes and Ladder, you will discover that you can be on square sixty and end up at zero. Does it mean you should stop playing? No. Life goes on. In playing Monopoly, you can have a dozen properties and end up in jail. It's time to collect rent and miss chances. It matters not how and why you fall; what matters most is how you pick yourself up from the gutter to attain your previous glory and beyond, so that your later glory shines brighter than the first. Job received ten times more at the end than he had at the beginning. There is growth and maturity in failure.

Every master needs to master failure too and graduate with distinctions. Enjoy living with plenty, and endure living with little. Joy comes in the morning, after a night soiled in tears. Masters are not ashamed to share the life paths they have experienced; they have learned to open the books of their lives for others to follow.

Masters are the reference books of life. At every turn, there is a lesson for another traveler on this highway of life. The entire community asks what we should do when we pass through such such perilous times. The life of a master is a portrait of encouragement on walls made of questions, an encyclopedia of acronyms for sophomores in life, a dictionary of a foreign language for the quick reference of a traveler who has come from afar. So you want to be a master? Don't show only one side of life—success—tell us about both the upside and the downside of it.

Parents, don't try to live a supernatural life for your children by protecting them from error and pain. Share life in its totality with your offspring. Fairy homes only exist in Disneyland.

I love my parents, and I can share this: I have never seen them fight or argue in front of me ever since I was born. I am now the father of two children. My wife and I have our differences, and I discover that my dictionary is blank and my tool box is empty. All I remember is Mum and Dad going into a bedroom for a few moments and then coming out smiling. Now I am in that bedroom, and I don't know what to do or say. Very few times do I come out of that room smiling.

Share some of your life with your children, and you will see the result at the end. Share pain and joy with your kids. It will do them well to learn some tips from you, especially about how you repair your life after a loss. I shun a community that shields its kids, making them grow in cocoons, ill-equipped and paralyzed for life.

So you want to be a master? Make masters, and make your life a clear illustration from which they can draw strength and examples. Tell your children when you made a mistake. Tell your son when you did not treat his mother right. Tell your daughter that that is not how you should treat your man. The impact is great if kids learn from their parents. Tell them what works, and show them what destroys. Show them the scars that you got on the highway. Show them how to treat other people and how to run an inn.

Learning is continuous, and all parties are growing. Our children will do it better than we did. As parents do this, they must admit that they don't know everything, and in sharing, they become strong and build the confidence of their children in the reality of marriage and life itself. Children are not born in heaven, and they know they are not living with angelic parents. Prepare the next generation to live on Earth and not destroy it.

In business, you are not a superpower carrying weapons of mass destruction, performing miracles with wonder-making powers. Masters, impart your visions, goals, and dreams as leaders, not as bosses. Demonstrate the way as you walk it; don't load it on your workers because you pay them. The worst employee is the one who just works for his or her money, meeting only the bare minimum of requirements.

Distribute the profits of success and the reductions of losses. If it is done truthfully, you will develop loyal employees who believe in your brand more than the customer. Nothing kills a good brand more than good marketing. Where the custodians and producers of a brand don't believe in the ethics of their brand, as they rub shoulders with customers, they send a different signal. It's your duty as a master to get them to buy and utilize the brand.

A community is full of suspicion when they know you work at the bakery but never buy the brand of the bread you bake. It says a lot about the hygiene and other issues. In my tribe, it is the best example of brand essence. When you bring me water to quench thirst, you are the one to drink it first. If there is poison, you die first. We actually call it "taking out the medicine." Live and lead by example.

We eat in a circle, using the same dish. One of the African maxims says that "a big person doesn't clean up the plates with the small fellows." Put another way, when you have eaten, though you are not full, and if you notice that the food is getting finished, leave the youngsters to clean up. I should think that pilots are trained from my tribal ethical practice. A pilot is taught to abandon the aircraft last, after doing all that he or she can do to save the passengers and the crew.

This principle needs to filter into the business environment. Why? Because each time there is a financial problem, the first cut is on employees. As a master, lay down your life for your flock. Some of the salaries we take home can save an entire division. Leaders need to have people at heart more than profits.

Reflections

- How does it feel to walk past a person in pain and do nothing about it?
- Do you know people who need your help and care?
- How do you formulate your thoughts?

Applications

- Look at the empty geometric chart presented here and complete your envelope, focusing mainly on areas where you need to build.

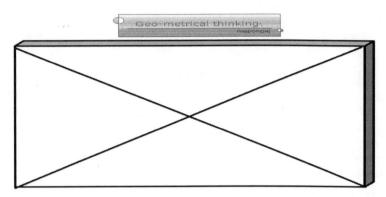

Which sphere or line is the most challenging to you, and what plan of action have you put in place to regain strength?

- Do good deeds today. Identify a disadvantaged person, take him or her to the best restaurant, and diarize his or her emotions.
- Nurse others in pain, and see how it heals your pain.
- Find books or experts who can help you develop the weak sphere or line. Most importantly, place and consult God first, before everything.

CONCLUSION

Practical Lifestyle Guide for a
NEW START

These are the fundamental roots and ingredients for the master:

Nutrition: What you eat is what you are. Every master has a diet that he follows, for there is a very close link between food and performance. Your diet will affect your brain activity.

Exercise: Find some form of physical exercise that will help improve the circulation of blood and breathing. A few minutes per day—a small walk, jog, or work in the garden, just to sweat a little bit and increase your heart rate—will yield a good result. Make it a lifestyle, and build it into your system.

Water: The medical profession recommends seven glasses of water per day. Isn't it amazing that 70 percent of the world is water and our bodies are 70 percent water too? Yes, there are lots of nice drinks and concoctions, but water is the best. Find a clean source of water, and make it your daily drink. Don't forget that you also need it for external use; love water, bathe, and make this a ritual. Water is therapeutic.

Sunshine: Open windows every morning, and allow the sun to greet your linen. Work in an environment that has as much sunlight as possible. Darkness is depressing, and light is encouraging. While in the UK, I was very depressed, particularly in winter when I was on the Tube, heated against the snow outside. It was dark inside, and no one was talking. All faces were buried in newspapers and books. Come summer, people were bubbling with songs in their hearts. I used to miss my motherland, where there are twelve months of sunshine and where we walk with our heads up, wearing few clothes, unlike the mobile wardrobes of cold lands. Avoid thick and heavy curtains that cover the windows and even the walls of your office or your bedroom; they detract from the sunbeams.

Temperance: Moderate use of good and total abstinence from evil: this principle governs all spheres of a master's life. Do everything in moderation. Avoid all extremes. Temperance is the main hub of a balanced life. This will moderate all practices, thoughts, emotions, physical expenditure, and mental exertion. Let the master practice temperance uncompromisingly, at all costs.

Air: Lots of fresh air is life. It is a pity that there are thieves and high crime and that people resort to shutting windows, especially during the night. In principle, windows must not be completely closed, for at night, people breathe stale air and leave a small space to allow in fresh air. Walk in the open fields, and take deep breaths of clean air.

Rest: Have adequate sleep. The body is a fascinating machine; we are awesomely and wonderfully made. When fatigue kicks in, the body will shut down and reduce its output. The best way to refresh yourself is not by taking pills to stay awake. Just take a nice walk, have a nice bath, and sleep. While you are asleep, the body will reboot your system and reformat your hard drive. It is hard for some people to part with work or entertainment, watching movies till dawn on daily basis. Yes, you can do it, but it is not healthy and good for masters. Give your body ample rest, to build up your strength for another day.

Trust: Finally, masters are trustworthy, and they invest in trusting people. This feels like a no-no in business, but a master must not lose hope in the human spirit. Trust people. It's not how they respond, but how it positions you in their lives. Put backup plans in place, but hey, without trust, you will not delegate work, empower, or employ. Have faith in

God and also in yourself, and be patient with others. Give them second chances. Run a repair shop for broken spirits. Reintroduce people to their spirits by emphasizing how much better they can do, rather than how badly they have failed. In most cases, people will change for good in an environment of positive reinforcement.

THE END

References and Notes

Key Source: *The Bible: NIV* (Thompson chain reference Seventh Edition)

Warren Keegan and Hugh Davidson. *Offensive Marketing: An Action Guide to Gaining Competitive Advantage,* Elservier: Butterworth-Heinemann, 2005 The five key principles of Offensive Marketing—Profitable, Offensive, Integrated, Strategic, and Effectively Executed, as summarized in the mnemonic POISE—provide the basis for this book and the roadmap for building an effective and successful marketing program across an organization and its partners.

Wolpert Stanley, *Gandhi's Passion: Life and Legacy of Mahatma Gandhi,* Delhi, Oxford University Press, 2001. A reminder of an extraordinary life and a great soul. Almost sixty years after his death, Ghandi still inspires millions. His legacy moved the heart of Martin Luther King Jr., and he was an icon to Nelson Mandela.

Anthony Sampson, *The Authorized Biography,* Harper Collins, 1999. He spent twenty-five years behind bars and had a "long walk to freedom." This authorized biography is an insight into understanding an enigmatic and private person who is noted as one of the century's greatest men.

Clayborne Carson, (Editor). *The Autobiography of Martin Luther King Jr..* New York: Warner Books, 1998. A mild-mannered, inquisitive man who stood to rebel against segregation. A loving father and devoted husband who sought to balance his family life with his involvement in a demanding nationwide movement of human rights. He had a dream for

America and humanity. He died having seen the promised land, the glory of the coming of the Lord.

Gillian Butler and Tony Hope, *Manage Your Mind*, UK, Oxford University Press, 2007

F. E. Belden, *Hark, the Voice of Jesus Is Calling* Seventh-day Adventist Hymnody, IAMA, 1981

Desmond Morris, *The Naked Ape: A Zoologist's Study of the Human Animal*, McGraw-Hill Companies, USA & Canada 1967. Desmond Morris looks at humans as a species and compares them to other animals. He depicts human behavior as partially evolved to meet the challenges of prehistoric life as a hunter-gatherer (nature versus nurture).

Author: Maponga Joshua III "Vhudzijena"

Joshua is an acclaimed, successful social entrepreneur living in South Africa with a keen passion for community development. His experience was gained in working with organizations such as EDSA (Entrepreneurial Development Southern Africa), the Seventh-day Adventist Church, Global Management Centre (UK), and Vision Design House. He holds a degree in philosophy topped up with CET (Construction Entrepreneurial Training) and ILO (International Labour Organisation) initiative to develop local consultants and support for emerging contractors and manufacturers. Within this crucial environment of the twenty-first century, his abilities range from creative intellectual power to pragmatic thinking, and he has a keen interest in in-depth thinking, behavioural patterns, and paradigmatic shifts in mindsets. He has managed major brands in South Africa and has earned a reputation, both locally and internationally, through his excellent spirited and entrepreneurial presentations. He is well traveled, with diverse innovative skills informed by his effective communication.

978-0-595-45567-6
0-595-45567-0

Made in the USA
Columbia, SC
05 May 2019